FRENCH VOCABULARY WORKBOOK

50 French Vocabulary Activities for Daily Practice

DYLANE MOREAU

ISBN: 978-1-998024-18-6

TABLE OF CONTENTS

PREFACE

Welcome to the *French Vocabulary Workbook*, a carefully designed resource for high beginners to intermediate learners of French. This workbook features 50 engaging activities focusing on key vocabulary topics such as the house, transportation, expressions, animals, etc. Each chapter helps you expand your vocabulary in practical, everyday contexts, allowing you to build your confidence and fluency in French.

The activities in this workbook are made into bite-size lessons, allowing you to practice French daily even when you have little time for your learning journey.

The exercises are easy to follow, making daily practice simple and effective. With a variety of activities, you'll not only learn new words but also understand how to use them in context. To support your progress, the book includes an answer key and free downloadable audio to help you improve your listening and pronunciation skills.

This workbook is part of the larger series, including the *French Grammar Workbook* and *French Listening Workbook*, providing a comprehensive approach to mastering French. Whether you're studying on your own or supplementing classroom lessons, this workbook is a valuable tool for practicing and refining your French vocabulary.

I hope this book becomes an essential part of your language-learning journey. Happy learning!

Dylane

HOW TO USE THIS BOOK

This book is designed to improve your French vocabulary with different subjects of daily life. To maximize your learning experience, here are some helpful tips:

- Take advantage of the note pages throughout the book. Keep track of the vocabulary you learned, the questions you got right and the ones you got wrong. Come back to your notes often to review them.
- Pace Yourself: Instead of doing all the lessons and exercises in one sitting, try focusing on one chapter and one subject per day. Since this book includes 50 chapters, you will have 50 days of French practice.
- Do the Exercises: Each chapter ends with an exercise to practice what you just learned or reviewed. The exercises are not translated into English under the sentence, as I usually do. This time, the translation is further down in the chapter. It's there if you need it, but it's not directly with the French sentence to make you think about the vocabulary.
- Improve Your Listening Skills: Take advantage of the free audio download and listen to each activity while simultaneously reading the text. This technique will help you connect spoken and written French and may improve your pronunciation.

That's it! Let's learn new French vocabulary!

Have fun learning!

HOW TO USE THE VOCABULARY LISTS

Each vocabulary list contains the relevant words for the topic and is presented following the lesson.

To optimize your learning experience, here are some important things to consider when using the vocabulary list:

- Whenever possible, all nouns are converted to their singular form so you can easily recognize their gender. Some nouns, such as profession, have masculine and feminine forms.
- All adjectives are presented in both masculine and feminine forms.
- Verbs are listed in their infinitive form to help you recognize their base form.
- Additionally, each vocabulary word is accompanied by its part of speech when possible, which is indicated in the legend below.

Legend

adj – adjective	**adjectif**
adv – adverb	**adverbe**
n – noun	**nom** (when both genders are given)
nf – feminine noun	**nom féminin**
nm – masculine noun	**nom masculin**
prép – preposition	**préposition**
pp – past participle	**participe présent**
v – verb	**verbe**

HOW TO DOWNLOAD THE AUDIO

To download the audio files of all the recordings in this book, visit

www.theperfectfrench.com/french-vocabulary-workbook-audios

or scan the QR code below.

After entering your email, the link for the audio download will be sent directly to your inbox with step-by-step instructions. If you encounter an issue, please send me an email at **info@theperfectfrench.com**

LES PIÈCES DE LA MAISON
ROOMS OF THE HOUSE

1

AUDIO 1.1

Un atelier nm | *A workshop*
Une bibliothèque nf | *A library*
Une buanderie nf | *A laundry room*
Un bureau nm | *An office*
Une cave nf | *A cellar*
Une chambre d'amis nf | *A guest room*
Une chambre nf | *A bedroom*
Un couloir nm | *A hallway*
Une cuisine nf | *A kitchen*
Un débarras nm | *A storage room*
Un dressing nm | *A walk-in closet*

Un garage nm | *A garage*
Un grenier nm | *An attic*
Un hall d'entrée nm | *An entrance*
Une salle à manger nf | *A dining room*
Une salle de bain nf | *A bathroom*
Une salle de jeux nf | *A playroom*
Un salon nm | *A living room*
Une terrasse nm | *A patio*
Les toilettes nf | *A toilet – A powder room*
Une véranda nf | *A solarium*

AUDIO 1.2

Ajoutez **la bonne pièce** à chaque phrase.
Add the correct room to each sentence.

1. Je dors dans ma   .

2. Je prépare mes repas dans la   .

3. Je fais ma lessive dans la   .

4. Je me lave dans la   .

5. Je range le balai dans le   .

6. Je travaille dans mon   .

7. Quand mes amis me rendent visite, ils dorment dans la   .

8. Le soir, je gare ma voiture dans le   .

9. Mes habits sont rangés dans le   .

10. Mes bouteilles de vin sont à la   .

11. Je regarde la télévision dans le _____ .

12. Les enfants jouent dans la _____ .

 Questions personnelles.
Personal questions.

13. La pièce que je préfère chez moi : _____

14. La pièce que j'aime le moins chez moi : _____

15. La pièce que j'aimerais avoir chez moi : _____

TRANSLATION

1. *I sleep in my bedroom.*
2. *I prepare my meals in the kitchen.*
3. *I do my laundry in the laundry room.*
4. *I shower in the bathroom.*
5. *I put the broom in the storage room.*
6. *I work in my office.*
7. *When my friends visit me, they sleep in the guest room.*
8. *In the evening, I park my car in the garage.*
9. *My clothes are stored in the walk-in closet.*
10. *My bottles of wine are in the cellar.*
11. *I watch television in the living room.*
12. *The children play in the playroom.*
13. *My favorite room in my home:*
14. *My least favorite room in my home:*
15. *The room I would like to have in my home:*

LES VÊTEMENTS
CLOTHING

2

Acheter v | *To buy*
Commander en ligne v | *To order online*
Échanger v | *To exchange*
Enlever v | *To take off*
Essayer v | *To try on*
Faire du shopping v | *To shop*
Laver v | *To wash*
Mettre v | *To put on*
Porter v | *To wear*
Retourner v | *To return*
S'habiller v | *To get dressed*
Se changer v | *To get changed*
Se déshabiller v | *To get undressed*

Des chaussettes nf | *Socks*
Des chaussures nf | *Shoes*
Une chemise nf | *A shirt*
Un gilet nm | *A cardigan*
Une jupe nf | *A skirt*
Un legging nm | *A pair of leggings*
Un pantalon nm | *Pants*
Un pull nm | *A sweater*
Une robe nf | *A dress*
Un short nm | *Shorts*
Un t-shirt nm | *A t-shirt*
Une taille nf | *A size*
Un top nm | *A top*

Trop petit – petite | *Too small*
Trop grand – grande | *Too big – Too large*
Mal taillé(e) | *Badly cut*

Des baskets nf | *Sneakers*
Des bottes nf | *Boots*
Des chaussures à talons nf | *High-heel shoes*
Des chaussures plates nf | *Flat-heel shoes*
Une pointure nf | *A shoesize*
Des sandales nf | *Sandals*
Des tongs nf | *Flip-flops*

 Complétez les phrases avec **le vocabulaire** ci-dessous.
Complete the sentences with the vocabulary below.

essayer – baskets – pointure – acheter – tongs – faire du shopping – chaussures –
taille – ai commandé – robe – petit – gilet – taillé – s'habille – bottes

1. Quelle est votre   ?

2. J'   des vêtements en ligne.

3. Mets ton   si tu as froid.

---

essayer – baskets – pointure – acheter – tongs – faire du shopping – chaussures – taille – ai commandé – robe – petit – gilet – taillé – s'habille – bottes

4. On _____ toujours avant de prendre notre petit déjeuner.

5. Mes _____ sont pleines de boue.

6. Cette _____ te va très bien.

7. Tu as pris tes _____ pour courir ?

8. C'est bien de porter des _____ à la piscine.

9. Il faut toujours _____ avant d'acheter.

10. Ce pantalon est mal _____ .

11. Je dois faire réparer mes _____ pour l'hiver.

12. On va _____ ce week-end.

13. Ce manteau est trop _____ pour toi.

14. Est-ce que vous avez la _____ au-dessus ?

15. Je pense _____ un nouveau pull pour mes vacances.

TRANSLATION

1. *What is your shoe size?*
2. *I ordered clothes online.*
3. *Put on your cardigan if you are cold.*
4. *We always get dressed before having breakfast.*
5. *My shoes are full of mud.*
6. *This dress suits you very well.*
7. *Did you take your sneakers to run?*
8. *It's good to wear flip flops to the pool.*
9. *Always try before you buy.*
10. *These pants are poorly tailored.*
11. *I need to get my boots repaired for the winter.*
12. *We're going shopping this weekend.*
13. *This coat is too small for you.*
14. *Do you have a larger size?*
15. *I'm thinking of buying a new sweater for my vacation.*

LES RÉSEAUX SOCIAUX
SOCIAL MEDIA

3

Un abonné – Une abonnée n | *A subscriber*
Un abonnement nm | *A subscription*
Une application – Une appli nf |
An application – An app
Une chaîne nf | *A channel*
Un commentaire nm | *A comment*
Un compte nm | *An account*
Le contenu nm | *The content*
Une demande d'ami nf | *A friend request*
Un emoji nm | *An emoji*
En ligne adj | *Online*
Un groupe nm | *A group*
Un fil d'actualité nm | *A wall – A feed*
Hors ligne adj | *Offline*
Un lien nm | *A link*
Un nom d'utilisateur nm | *A username*
Une photo de couverture nf | *A cover picture*
Une photo de profil nf | *A profile picture*
Une photo nf | *A picture*

Un profil nm | *A profile*
Une publication nf | *A post*
Un réseau social nm | *A social media*
Une story nf | *A story*
Une tendance nf | *A trend*
Une vidéo nf | *A video*

S'abonner v | *To subscribe*
Se désabonner v | *To unsubscribe*
Bloquer v | *To block*
Se connecter v | *To log in*
Se déconnecter v | *To log out*
Discuter v | *To talk*
Naviguer v | *To navigate*
Partager v | *To share*
Poster v | *To post*
Publier v | *To publish*
Réagir v | *To react*
Suivre v | *To follow*

 Choisissez entre **les deux mots donnés** pour chaque phrase.
Choose between the two words given for each sentence.

1. **vidéo – lien** – Est-ce que tu as vu la _____ que je viens de publier ?

2. **tendance – demande d'ami** – Tu n'as pas reçu ma _____ ?

3. **abonné – émoji** – Elle ajoute toujours un _____ à la fin de ses phrases.

4. **abonnés – groupes** – Son compte Instagram a 2000 _____ .

5. **compte – chaîne** – Je n'ai jamais regardé sa _____ YouTube.

6. **lien – nom d'utilisateur** – L'auteur a partagé le _____ de son livre dans sa story.

7. **bloqué – en ligne** – Je vois qu'il est ⬚⬚⬚⬚⬚ mais il ne me répond pas.

8. **commentaire – photo de profil** – Elle veut changer sa ⬚⬚⬚⬚⬚ mais elle ne trouve pas de belle photo.

9. **nom d'utilisateur – réseau social** – Quel est ton ⬚⬚⬚⬚⬚ ?

10. **applications – groupe** – Combien d' ⬚⬚⬚⬚⬚ est-ce que vous utilisez ?

11. **chaîne – compte** – Mon ⬚⬚⬚⬚⬚ est bloqué mais je ne sais pas pourquoi.

12. **commentaires – tendances** – On aime lire les ⬚⬚⬚⬚⬚ en-dessous de nos photos.

13. **groupes – comptes** – Ma mère est dans plusieurs ⬚⬚⬚⬚⬚ Facebook.

14. **vidéo – fil d'actualité** – Il n'y a rien de nouveau sur mon ⬚⬚⬚⬚⬚ .

15. **discute – navigue** – Je ⬚⬚⬚⬚⬚ avec beaucoup de gens en ligne.

TRANSLATION

1. *Did you see the video I just posted?*
2. *Didn't you receive my friend request?*
3. *She always adds an emoji at the end of her sentences.*
4. *His Instagram account has 2000 subscribers.*
5. *I have never watched her YouTube channel.*
6. *The author shared the link to his book in his story.*
7. *I see he is online but he doesn't answer me.*
8. *She wants to change her profile photo but she can't find a nice photo.*
9. *What is your username?*
10. *How many apps do you use?*
11. *My account is blocked but I don't know why.*
12. *We like reading the comments below our photos.*
13. *My mother is in several Facebook groups.*
14. *There's nothing new on my news feed.*
15. *I chat with a lot of people online.*

LES IMMEUBLES ET LES MAGASINS
BUILDINGS AND SHOPS

4

AUDIO 4.1 🔊

Les immeubles – Buildings

Un aéroport nm | *An airport*
Une bibliothèque nf | *A library*
Un bureau de poste nm | *A post office*
Une école nf | *A school*
Une gare nf | *A train station*
Un gratte-ciel nm | *A skyscraper*
Un hôpital nm | *A hospital*
L'hôtel de ville – La mairie n | *City Hall*
Un hôtel nm | *A hotel*
Un immeuble à appartements nm | *An apartment building*
Un immeuble de bureaux nm | *An office building*
Une librairie nf | *A bookstore*
Un petit magasin nm | *A convenience store*
Un poste de police nm | *A police station*
Une prison nf | *A jail*
Une tour nf | *A tower*
Un tribunal nm | *Court*
Une usine nf | *A factory*

AUDIO 4.2 🔊

Les magasins – Shops

Une boucherie nf | *A butcher*
Une boulangerie nf | *A bakery*
Un café nm | *A cafe*
Un centre commercial nm | *A shopping center*
Un fleuriste nm | *A flower shop*
Une épicerie nf | *A grocery store*
Une librairie nf | *A bookstore*
Un magasin de chaussures nm | *A shoe store*
Un magasin de jouets nm | *A toy store*
Un magasin de musique nm | *A music store*
Un magasin de seconde main nm | *A thrift store*
Un magasin de spiritueux nm | *A liquor store*

Un magasin de sport nm | *A sports store*
Un magasin de vêtements nm | *A clothes store*
Une pâtisserie nf | *A bakery*
Une pharmacie nf | *A pharmacy*
Une pizzéria nf | *A pizza parlor*
Un restaurant nm | *A restaurant*
Un salon de coiffure nm | *A hairdresser*
Une station d'essence nf | *A petrol station – A gas station*
Un supermarché nm | *A supermarket*

AUDIO 4.3

 Utilisez la liste ci-dessus pour trouver **le bon immeuble** ou **magasin** pour chaque phrase.
Use the list above to find the correct building or store for each sentence.

1. Je dois être à l'   dans deux heures pour prendre mon avion.

2. Le criminel sera jugé au   .

3. Elle fait toujours ses courses au   du coin.

4. Ils viennent d'acheter un appartement tout en haut de ce   .

5. Est-ce que tu peux aller à la   pour aller chercher ses médicaments ?

6. J'aime habiter à côté d'une   car ma maison sent toujours le pain.

7. La   a des promotions sur le blanc de poulet.

8. Les enfants vont à la   pour lire des histoires.

9. Nous avons passé nos vacances dans un   près de la plage.

10. Tu dois aller chercher ton colis au   aujourd'hui.

11. Elle doit s'arrêter à la   car sa voiture n'a plus d'essence.

12. Mon père travaille dans une   de papier.

13. J'ai commandé un énorme beaucoup de roses chez le   .

14. On peut trouver de bonnes affaires au .

15. Je vais boire un verre avec mon mari au après le travail.

TRANSLATION

1. *I have to be at the airport in two hours to catch my plane.*
2. *The criminal will be tried in court.*
3. *She always shops at the local supermarket/mall.*
4. *They just bought an apartment at the top of this skyscraper.*
5. *Can you go to the pharmacy to get his medication?*
6. *I like living next to a bakery because my house always smells of bread.*
7. *The butcher shop has promotions on chicken breast.*
8. *The children go to the library to read stories.*
9. *We spent our vacation in a hotel near the beach.*
10. *You need to pick up your package at the post office today.*
11. *She has to stop at the gas station because her car is out of gas.*
12. *My father works in a paper factory.*
13. *I ordered a huge bouquet of roses from the florist.*
14. *You can find good deals at the second-hand store.*
15. *I'm going to have a drink with my husband at the cafe after work.*

DÉCRIVEZ-VOUS

DESCRIBE YOURSELF

5

Décrivez-vous en répondant aux questions suivantes. Mes propres réponses sont dans les solutions.
Describe yourself by answering the following questions. My own answers are in the solutions.

1. Comment vous appelez-vous ?

2. Quel âge avez-vous ?

3. Quand est votre anniversaire ?

4. Où est-ce que vous habitez ?

5. Qu'est-ce que vous faites dans la vie ?

6. Est-ce que vous avez des frères et sœurs ?

7. De quelle couleur sont vos cheveux ?

8. Combien est-ce que vous mesurez ?

9. À quelle heure est-ce que vous vous levez ?

10. Qu'est-ce que vous aimez faire pendant votre temps libre ?

11. Quel est votre fruit préféré ?

12. Quelle est votre boisson préférée ?

13. Est-ce que vous avez des animaux de compagnie ?

14. Quelle(s) langue(s) est-ce que vous parlez ?

15. À quelle heure est-ce que vous vous couchez tous les soirs ?

TRANSLATION

1. *What is your name?*
2. *How old are you?*
3. *When is your birthday?*
4. *Where do you live?*
5. *What do you do for a living?*
6. *Do you have brothers and sisters?*
7. *What's the color of your hair?*
8. *How tall are you?*
9. *What time do you get up?*
10. *What do you like to do in your free time?*
11. *What is your favorite fruit ?*
12. *What is your favorite drink?*
13. *Do you have pets?*
14. *What language(s) do you speak?*
15. *What time do you go to bed every night?*

MOTS FLÉCHÉS – MON ANNIVERSAIRE
CROSSWORD – MY BIRTHDAY

6

Below you can find 35 words related to a birthday. Read and study the vocabulary before filling up the crossword or challenge yourself and try directly the crossword.

AUDIO 6.1 ◀))

Un ami – Une amie n | *A friend*
Un an nm | *A year*
Un anniversaire nm | *A birthday*
Un ballon nm | *A balloon*
Boire v | *To drink*
Un bonbon nm | *A candy*
Une bougie nf | *A candle*
Un cadeau nm | *A gift*
Une carte nf | *A card*
Chanter v | *To sing*
Un clown nm | *A clown*
Couper v | *To cut*
Une danse nf | *A dance*
Les décorations nf | *Decorations*
Un emballage nm | *Wrap*
Une famille nf | *A family*
Une fête nf | *A party*
Fêter v | *To celebrate*
Un gâteau nm | *A cake*
Une invitation nf | *An invitation*
Un invité – Une invitée n | *A guest*
Un jeu nm | *A game*
Un magicien nm | *A magician*
Manger v | *To eat*
De la musique nf | *Music*
Un nœud nm | *A bow*
Offrir v | *To give*
Organiser v | *To organize*
Une photo nf | *A photo*
Recevoir v | *To receive*
S'amuser v | *To have a good time*
Souffler v | *To blow*
Un souvenir nm | *A memory*
Une surprise nf | *A surprise*
Un vœu nm | *A wish*

Ajoutez la traduction de chaque mot dans **les cases numérotées**. Pour les noms, ajoutez seulement le nom et pas l'article.

Add the translation of each word in the numbered boxes. For nouns, add only the noun and not the article.

ACROSS

1. photo
2. to cut
3. birthday
4. to drink

5. to organize
6. cake
7. family
8. to eat

DOWN

9. gift
10. invitation
11. game
12. wrap

13. candy
14. to blow
15. to sing

LES COULEURS
COLORS

7

AUDIO 7.1 🔊

Beige adj | *Beige*
Blanc – Blanche adj | *White*
Bleu – Bleue adj | *Blue*
Brun – Brune – Marron adj | *Brown*
Gris – Grise adj | *Grey*
Jaune adj | *Yellow*

Noir – Noire adj | *Black*
Orange adj | *Orange*
Rose adj | *Pink*
Rouge adj | *Red*
Vert – Verte adj | *Green*
Violet – Violette adj | *Violet – Purple*

Orange and marron don't agree in gender and numbers.

AUDIO 7.2 🔊

*Ajoutez **la bonne couleur** à chaque phrase.*
Add the correct color to each sentence.

1. La neige est   .

2. Les citrons sont   .

3. Le drapeau français est   ,   et
                   .

4. L'habit du Père Noël est   et   .

5. Il pleut, le ciel est   .

Exercice personnel – Ajoutez la couleur des choses autour de vous.
Personal exercise – Add the color of things around you.

6. Le mur devant moi est   .

7. Mon pull est   .

8. Ma bouteille d'eau est   .

9. La couverture sur mon lit est   .

10. Mon canapé est   .

TRANSLATION

1. *The snow is white.*

2. *Lemons are yellow.*

3. *The French flag is blue, white and red.*

4. *Santa's outfit is red and white.*

5. *It's raining, the sky is grey.*

6. *The wall in front of me is*   .

7. *My sweater is*   .

8. *My water bottle is*   .

9. *The blanket on my bed is*   .

10. *My sofa is*   .

50 EXPRESSIONS FRANÇAISES COURANTES

8

50 COMMON FRENCH EXPRESSIONS

AUDIO 8.1 ◀》

Expressions with Être – *To be*

Être + nationality – *To be + nationality*
Être de – *To be from*
Être à quelqu'un – *To belong to somebody*
Être à l'heure – *To be on time*
Être au courant – *To be informed*
Être d'accord – *To agree*
Être de bonne humeur – *To be in a good mood*
Être de retour – *To be back*
Être en avance – *To be early*
Être en retard – *To be late*
Être en colère – *To be angry*
Être en train de (+ inf) – *To be in the process of (doing)*
Être en bonne santé – *To be healthy*
Être sur le point de (+ inf) – *To be about to (do)*

AUDIO 8.2 ◀》

Expressions with Avoir – *To have*

Avoir ... ans – *To be ... years old*
Avoir faim – *To be hungry*
Avoir soif – *To be thirsty*
Avoir chaud – *To be hot*
Avoir froid – *To be cold*
Avoir sommeil – *To be sleepy*
Avoir peur – *To be afraid*
Avoir de la chance – *To be lucky*
Avoir besoin de – *To need*
Avoir envie de – *To want*
Avoir mal à + body part – *To have an ache*
Avoir mal à la tête – *To have a headache*
Avoir mal à la gorge – *To have a sore throat*
Avoir mal au ventre – *To have a stomach ache*
Avoir mal au dos – *To have back pain*
Avoir mal aux dents – *To have a toothache*

Expressions with Aller – *To go*

Aller + inf. – *To be going + inf.*
Aller à pied – *To go on foot*
Aller à quelqu'un – *To suit someone*
Allez (filler word) – *Come on – Let's go*

Expressions with Faire – *To do* | À la maison – *At home*

Faire la cuisine – *To cook*
Faire la lessive – *To do the laundry*
Faire la vaisselle – *To do the dishes*
Faire son lit – *To make one's bed*

Expressions with Faire – *To do* | À l'école – *At school*

Faire ses devoirs – *To do one's homework*
Faire des progrès – *To make progress*
Faire des fautes – *To make mistakes*

Expressions with Faire – *To do* | Le sport – *Sport*

Faire du sport – *To exercise*
Faire du vélo – *To bike*
Faire du football – *To play soccer*
Faire de la natation – *To swim*

Expressions with Faire – *To do* | Les loisirs – *Hobbies*

Faire une promenade – *To take a walk*
Faire un voyage – *To take a trip*

Expressions with Faire – *To do* | Le temps – *The weather*

Il fait chaud – *It's warm*
Il fait froid – *It's cold*

Other Expressions with Faire

Faire attention – *To pay attention*
Faire la tête – *To be moody*
Faire peur (à) – *To scare*

AUDIO 8.10 ◄))

 Ajoutez **la bonne expression** à chaque phrase.
Add the right expression to each sentence.

a de la chance – ai mal à la tête – ai mal aux dents – ai soif – es au courant –
est en bonne santé – faire la lessive – faire une promenade – fais attention – fais du sport –
fait chaud – fait des progrès – font leurs devoirs – suis en retard – va à pied

1. Je n'ai plus rien de propre. Je dois   .

2. Est-ce que tu   de la nouvelle ?

3. Elle a reçu les résultats de sa prise de sang. Elle   .

4. Il   avec son nouveau professeur.

5. Je n'ai pas bu d'eau aujourd'hui. J'   .

6. Est-ce que tu as un médicament pour la migraine ? J'   .

7.   de ne pas tomber en descendant de l'échelle.

8. Je dois aller chez le dentiste aujourd'hui car j'   .

9. On essaie de   tous les soirs après le dîner.

10. Il n'a pas de voiture donc il   au travail.

11. Les enfants   en rentrant de l'école.

12. Je   5 fois par semaine au minimum.

13. Il   d'avoir une belle maison.

14. Les températures ont atteint 40 degrés. Il   !

15. Je me suis levé en retard, je   .

TRANSLATION

1. *I don't have anything clean anymore. I have to do the laundry.*

2. *Have you heard the news?*

3. *She received the results of her blood test. She is healthy.*

4. *He is making progress with his new teacher.*

5. *I didn't drink any water today. I am thirsty.*

6. *Do you have any medication for migraine? I have a headache.*

7. *Be careful not to fall when going down the ladder.*

8. *I have to go to the dentist today because my teeth hurt.*

9. *We try to take a walk every evening after dinner.*

10. *He doesn't have a car so he walks to work.*

11. *The children do their homework when they come home from school.*

12. *I exercise at least 5 times a week.*

13. *He is lucky to have a nice house.*

14. *Temperatures reached 40 degrees. It's hot!*

15. *I got up late, I'm late.*

25 HOMOPHONES COURANTS

25 COMMON HOMOPHONES

Homophones are word that are pronounced the same but have different meanings. They can even have the same spelling sometimes. In this lesson, we are looking at 25 common French homophones.

AUDIO 9.1 🔊

Une amande nf | *An almond*
Une amende nf | *A fine*

Un an nm | *A year*
En adv | *Some*
En prep | *To – In*

La boue nf | *Mud*
Un bout nm | *A piece*

Ça pr | *That*
Sa adj | *Her – His – Its*

Un car nm | *A bus*
Car conj | *For – Because*
Un quart nm | *A quarter*

Ce pr | *This*
Se pr | *Themselves*

Cent n | *One hundred*
Le sang nm | *Blood*
Sans prep | *Without*

Comptant adj | *Cash*
Content adj | *Happy*

Le cou nm | *Neck*
Le coup nm | *Shot*
Le coût nm | *Cost*

Le cygne nm | *Swan*
Le signe nm | *Sign*

Dans prep | *In*
Une dent nf | *A tooth*

Une ancre nf | *An anchor*
De l'encre nf | *Ink*

La faim nf | *Hunger*
La fin nf | *End*

Le fard (à paupières) nm | *Make-up*
Un phare nm | *A lighthouse*

La foi nf | *Faith*
Le foie nm | *Liver*
Une fois nf | *Once – One time*

Un gène nm | *A gene*
La gêne nf | *Embarrassment*

Le hockey nm | *Hockey*
Le hoquet nm | *Hiccup*

Il pr | *He – It*
Ils pr | *They*

La art | *The*
La pr | *Her – It*
Là adv | *Here – There*

Un lac nm | *A lake*
La laque nf | *Hairspray*

Laid adj | *Ugly*
Le lait nm | *Milk*

Leur adj | *Their*
Leur pr | *Theirs – Them*
L'heure | *Hour*

Le maire nm | *Mayor*
La mer nf | *Sea*
La mère nf | *Mother*

Mai nm | *May*
Mais conj | *But*
Mes adj | *My*
Un mets nm | *A dish – A delicacy*

Le maître nm | *Master*
Mettre v | *To put*

 AUDIO 9.2

Choisissez entre **les deux homophones** pour chaque phrase.
Choose between the two homophones for each sentence.

1. **an – en** – Mon fils va avoir un _____ dans une semaine.

2. **laid – lait** – Est-ce que tu peux acheter du _____ au magasin avant de rentrer ?

3. **hockey – hoquet** – Il joue au _____ 3 fois par semaine depuis qu'il est petit.

4. **Il – Ils** – _____ ont reçu mon message mais ils ne m'ont pas répondu.

5. **dans – dent** – Mon téléphone est resté _____ la voiture.

6. **lac – laque** – Le _____ est presque vide à cause de la sécheresse.

7. **faim – fin** – La _____ du film était tellement triste !

8. **Sang – Sans** – _____ toi je ne suis rien.

9. **amendes – amandes** – Je préfère le lait d'_____.

10. **bout – boue** – Est-ce que tu veux un _____ de gâteau ?

11. **comptant – content** – Il était vraiment _____ de te voir.

12. **cou – coup** – Elle s'est fait mal au _____ en jouant au basket.

13. **signes – cygnes** – Il y a des _____ autour du lac.

14. **la – là** – Tu seras _____ ce soir ?

15. **mai – mais** – Ma fille est née au mois de _____ .

TRANSLATION

1. *My son will be one year old in a week.*
2. *Can you buy some milk at the store before you come home?*
3. *He has been playing hockey 3 times a week since he was little.*
4. *They received my message, but they did not answer me.*
5. *My phone remained in the car.*
6. *The lake is almost empty due to drought.*
7. *The ending of the film was so sad!*
8. *Without you I am nothing.*
9. *I prefer almond milk.*
10. *Do you want a piece of cake?*
11. *He was really happy to see you.*
12. *She hurt her neck while playing basketball.*
13. *There are swans around the lake.*
14. *You will be here tonight?*
15. *My daughter was born in May.*

VRAI OU FAUX
TRUE OR FALSE

10

Voici **20 faits** de connaissance générale. Écrivez **Vrai (V)** ou **Faux (F)** devant chaque phrase. Le vocabulaire est listé après l'exercice.
Here are 20 facts about common knowledge. Write Vrai (V) or Faux (F) in front of each sentence. The vocabulary is listed after the exercise.

1. _____ La tour Eiffel est située à Paris.

2. _____ La Terre est la troisième planète du système solaire.

3. _____ Le Japon est connu pour sa production de fromage.

4. _____ Le Titanic a coulé en 1912.

5. _____ La capitale de l'Italie est Madrid.

6. _____ Les chiens sont des mammifères.

7. _____ L'eau gèle à 0 degrés Celsius.

8. _____ La Grande Muraille de Chine est visible depuis la Lune.

9. _____ Les chats ont quatre pattes.

10. _____ Les abeilles produisent du miel.

11. _____ Le mont Everest est le plus haut sommet du monde.

12. _____ Les serpents sont des animaux à sang chaud.

13. _____ La capitale de la France est Berlin.

14. _____ Le soleil se lève à l'est et se couche à l'ouest.

15. _____ Les pingouins peuvent voler.

16. _____ L'arc-en-ciel a sept couleurs distinctes.

17. _____ Les éléphants sont les plus gros mammifères terrestres.

18.   Le pôle Nord est le point le plus au sud de la Terre.

19.   La Lune tourne autour de la Terre.

20.   Les dauphins sont des poissons.

AUDIO 10.2 ◀)

VOCABULARY

La tour Eiffel nf | *The Eiffel Tower*
Être situé(e) v | *To be located*
La Terre nf | *Earth*
Une planète nf | *A planet*
Le système solaire nm | *Solar system*
Le Japon nm | *Japan*
Être connu(e) v | *To be known*
La production nf | *Production*
Du fromage nm | *Cheese*
Couler v | *To sink*
La capitale nf | *The capital*
L'Italie nf | *Italy*
Un chien nm | *A dog*
Un mammifère nm | *A mammal*
L'eau nf | *Water*
Geler v | *To freeze*
Un degré nm | *A degree*
La Grande Muraille de Chine nf | *The Great Wall of China*
Visible adj | *Visible*
La Lune nf | *The Moon*
Un chat nm | *A cat*
Une patte nf | *A paw*
Une abeille nf | *A bee*
Produire v | *To produce*
Du miel nm | *Honey*
Le mont Everest nm | *Mount Everest*
Haut – Haute adj | *High*
Un sommet nm | *A peak*
Un seprent nm | *A snake*
Un animal nm | *An animal*
Le sang nm | *Blood*
Chaud – Chaude adj | *Hot*
La France nf | *France*
Le soleil nm | *The sun*

Se lever v | *To rise*
L'est nm | *East*
Se coucher v | *To set*
L'ouest nm | *West*
Un pinguoin nm | *A penguin*
Voler v | *To fly*
Un arc-en-ciel nm | *A rainbow*
Une couleur nf | *A color*
Distinct – Distincte adj | *Distinct*
Un éléphant nm | *An elephant*
Terrestre adj | *Land*
Le pôle Nord nm | *The North Pole*
Le sud nm | *South*
Tourner v | *To turn*
Un dauphin nm | *A dolphin*
Un poisson nm | *A fish*

TRANSLATION

1. *The Eiffel Tower is located in Paris.*
2. *The Earth is the third planet in the solar system.*
3. *Japan is known for its cheese production.*
4. *The Titanic sank in 1912.*
5. *The capital of Italy is Madrid.*
6. *Dogs are mammals.*
7. *Water freezes at 0 degrees Celsius.*
8. *The Great Wall of China is visible from the Moon.*
9. *Cats have four legs.*
10. *Bees produce honey.*
11. *Mount Everest is the highest peak in the world.*
12. *Snakes are warm-blooded animals.*
13. *The capital of France is Berlin.*
14. *The sun rises in the east and sets in the west.*
15. *Penguins can fly.*
16. *The rainbow has seven distinct colors.*
17. *Elephants are the largest land mammals.*
18. *The North Pole is the southernmost point on Earth.*
19. *The moon orbits the Earth.*
20. *Dolphins are fish.*

LES JOURS, LES MOIS ET LES SAISONS

11

DAYS, MONTHS, AND SEASONS

AUDIO 11.1 ◄))

Les jours de la semaine – Days of the week

Lundi nm | *Monday*
Mardi nm | *Tuesday*
Mercredi nm | *Wednesday*
Jeudi nm | *Thursday*

Vendredi nm | *Friday*
Samedi nm | *Saturday*
Dimanche nm | *Sunday*

AUDIO 11.2 ◄))

Les mois de l'année – Months of the year

Le mois de ... | *The month of*
Janvier nm | *January*
Février nm | *February*
Mars nm | *March*
Avril nm | *April*
Mai nm | *May*
Juin nm | *June*

Juillet nm | *July*
Août nm | *August*
Septembre nm | *September*
Octobre nm | *October*
Novembre nm | *November*
Décembre nm | *December*

AUDIO 11.3 ◄))

Les saisons – Seasons

Le printemps nm | *Spring*
L'été nm | *Summer*

L'automne nm | *Autumn – Fall*
L'hiver nm | *Winter*

AUDIO 11.4 ◄))

 Complétez les phrases avec **le bon jour, le bon mois** ou **la bonne saison**.
Certaines phrases sont personnelles.
Complete the sentences with the correct day, month or season. Some sentences are personal.

1. Mon anniversaire est en   .

2. Mon jour préféré est le   .

3. Mon prochain rendez-vous est un ▨▨▨▨ .

4. Ma saison préférée est ▨▨▨▨ .

5. Noël est en ▨▨▨▨ et en ▨▨▨▨ .

6. Les feuilles changent de couleurs en ▨▨▨▨ .

7. Les enfants vont à l'école du ▨▨▨▨ au ▨▨▨▨ .

8. On partira en vacances en ▨▨▨▨ .

9. Aujourd'hui, on est ▨▨▨▨ .

10. ▨▨▨▨ est un jour de repos pour beaucoup de monde.

11. ▨▨▨▨ est le premier jour de la semaine.

12. La rentrée scolaire est en ▨▨▨▨ .

13. Le mois le plus court de l'année est le mois de ▨▨▨▨ .

14. Halloween est célébrée en ▨▨▨▨ .

15. Beaucoup d'élèves sont en vacances en ▨▨▨▨ et en ▨▨▨▨ .

TRANSLATION

1. *My birthday is in* ▨▨▨▨ .
2. *My favorite day is* ▨▨▨▨ .
3. *My next appointment is on a* ▨▨▨▨ .
4. *My favorite season is* ▨▨▨▨ .
5. *Christmas is in December and in winter.*
6. *The leaves change colors in fall.*
7. *The children go to school from Monday to Friday.*
8. *We're going on vacation in* ▨▨▨▨ .
9. *Today is* ▨▨▨▨ .
10. *Sunday is a day of rest for many people.*
11. *Monday is the first day of the week.*
12. *The start of the school year is in September.*
13. *The shortest month of the year is February.*
14. *Halloween is celebrated in October.*
15. *Many students are on vacation in July and August.*

LES FORMES
SHAPES

12

AUDIO 12.1 🔊

Les formes 2D – 2D shapes

Un carré nm | *A square*
Un cercle nm | *A circle*
Un cœur nm | *A heart*
Un croissant nm | *A crescent*
Une demi-lune nf | *A half-moon*
Une étoile nf | *A star*
Un losange nm | *A diamond*
Un ovale nm | *An oval*
Un rectangle nm | *A rectangle*
Un triangle nm | *A triangle*

AUDIO 12.2 🔊

Les formes 3D – 3D shapes

Un cône nm | *A cone*
Un cube nm | *A cube*
Un cylindre nm | *A cylinder*
Une pyramide nf | *A pyramid*
Une sphère nf | *A sphere*

AUDIO 12.3 🔊

Les polygones – Polygons

Un hexagone nm | *A hexagon*
Un pentagone nm | *A pentagon*
Un octogone nm | *An octagon*
Un trapèze nm | *A trapezoid*
Un parallélogramme nm | *A parallelogram*

AUDIO 12.4 🔊

 Ajoutez **la bonne forme** en regardant à la liste ci-dessus.
Add the correct shape by looking at the list above.

1. Un carré en 3D est un _____ .

2. Un triangle en 3D est une _____ .

3. Un cercle en 3D est une _____ .

4. Un _____ a quatre côtés égaux.

5. Un _____ a deux côtés longs et deux côtés courts.

6. Un   est une forme avec trois côtés.

7. Un   est une forme ronde sans côtés.

8. Un   a six côtés égaux.

9. Un   est en forme de lune.

10. Un   est une forme qui représente l'amour.

TRANSLATION

1. *A 3D square is a cube.*
2. *A 3D triangle is a pyramid.*
3. *A 3D circle is a sphere.*
4. *A square has four equal sides.*
5. *A rectangle has two long sides and two short sides.*
6. *A triangle is a shape with three sides.*
7. *A circle is a round shape with no sides.*
8. *A hexagon has six equal sides.*
9. *A crescent is shaped like a moon.*
10. *A heart is a shape that represents love.*

LE MATIN, L'APRÈS-MIDI ET LE SOIR

13

MORNING, AFTERNOON, AND EVENING

AUDIO 13.1

 Qu'est-ce que vous faites le matin, l'après-midi et le soir ? Écrivez **M pour matin, A pour après-midi** et **S pour soir** devant chaque phrase. Mes propres réponses dans les solutions.
What do you do in the morning, in the afternoon and in the evening? Write M for matin, A for après-midi, and S for soir in front of each sentence. My own answers in solutions.

1.   – J'étudie le français.

2.   – Je me lève tôt.

3.   – Je me brosse les dents.

4.   – Je prends une douche ou un bain.

5.   – Je passe du temps sur mon téléphone.

6.   – Je prends mon petit déjeuner.

7.   – Je me prépare pour la journée.

8.   – Je mets mon pyjama.

9.   – Je mets mon réveil pour le lendemain matin.

10.   – Je fais du sport.

11.   – Je prépare le dîner.

12.   – Je rentre du travail ou de l'école.

13.   – Je fais les courses.

14.   – Je prépare mes affaires pour le lendemain.

15.   – Je vérifie mes emails.

VOCABULARY

Étudier v | *To study*
Le français nm | *French*
Se lever v | *To get up*
Tôt adv | *Early*
Se brosser les dents | *To brush your teeth*
Prendre une douche | *To take a shower*
Prendre un bain | *To take a bath*
Passer du temps | *To spend time*
Un téléphone nm | *A phone*
Prendre son petit déjeuner | *To have breakfast*
Se préparer v | *To get ready*
Une journée nf | *A day*
Mettre v | *To put*
Un pyjama nm | *The pajamas*
Un réveil nm | *An alarm clock*
Le lendemain matin | *The next morning*
Faire du sport | *To exercise*
Préparer v | *To prepare*
Le dîner nm | *Dinner*
Rentrer v | *To come home*
Le travail nm | *Work*
L'école nf | *School*
Faire les courses | *To shop*
Préparer ses affaires | *To prepare things*
Vérifier v | *To verify*
Un email nm | *An email*

TRANSLATION

1. *I study French.*
2. *I get up early.*
3. *I brush my teeth.*
4. *I take a shower or a bath.*
5. *I spend time on my phone.*
6. *I have my breakfast.*
7. *I get ready for the day.*
8. *I put on my pajamas.*
9. *I set my alarm for the next morning.*
10. *I workout.*
11. *I prepare dinner.*
12. *I come home from work or school.*
13. *I shop.*
14. *I prepare my things for the next day.*
15. *I check my emails.*

LES PARTIES DU CORPS
BODY PARTS

14

AUDIO 14.1 ◀))

Le cou nm | *Neck*
Le dos nm | *Back*
Les fesses nf | *Buttocks*
La hanche nf | *Hip*
Le nombril nm | *Belly button*
La poitrine nf | *Chest*
Le sein nm | *Breast*
Le torse nm | *Torso*
Le ventre nm | *Stomach*
L'avant-bras nm | *Forearm*
Le bras nm | *Arm*
Le coude nm | *Elbow*
L'épaule nf | *Shoulder*
Le poignet nm | *Wrist*
La cheville nf | *Ankle*
La cuisse nf | *Thigh*
Le genou nm | *Knee*
La jambe nf | *Leg*
Le mollet nm | *Calf*
Le doigt de pied – L'orteil nm | *Toe*
Le pied nm | *Foot*
La plante du pied nf | *Base of the foot*
Le talon nm | *Heel*

Le doigt nm | *Finger*
Le pouce nm | *Thumb*
L'index nm | *Index*
Le majeur nm | *Middle finger*
L'annulaire nm | *Ring finger*
L'auriculaire nm | *Little finger*
La main nf | *Hand*
Les ongles nm | *Nails*
Une phalange nf | *A phalanx*
La paume nf | *Palm*
Un os nm | *A bone*
Le cerveau nm | *Brain*
Le cœur nm | *Heart*
L'estomac nm | *Stomach*
Le foie nm | *Liver*
L'intestin nm | *Intestine*
Les organes vitaux nm | *Vital organs*
Les organes génitaux nm | *Genitals*
Le pancréas nm | *Pancreas*
Les poumons nm | *Lungs*
Les reins nm | *Kidneys*
La vessie nf | *Bladder*

AUDIO 14.2 ◀))

 Choisissez entre **les deux parties du corps** pour chaque phrase.
Choose between the two body parts for each sentence.

1. **cerveau – dos** – Il s'est fait mal au _____ en portant cette boîte lourde.

2. **poignet – cheville** – Elle a beaucoup trop de bracelets au _____ .

3. **auriculaire – annulaire** – On porte son alliance à l'_____ .

4. **reins – estomac** – Les ⬜⬜⬜⬜ filtrent les toxines du corps.

5. **phalange – vessie** – Elle a une petite ⬜⬜⬜⬜ . Elle doit toujours aller aux toilettes.

6. **coudes – organes** – Ne mets pas tes ⬜⬜⬜⬜ sur la table.

7. **mollet – cerveau** – J'ai souvent des crampes au ⬜⬜⬜⬜ .

8. **ventre – épaule** – Son ⬜⬜⬜⬜ est douloureuse depuis son match de tennis.

9. **genoux – ongles** – Elle a toujours du vernis sur ses ⬜⬜⬜⬜ .

10. **poitrine – cuisse** – Il faut aller à l'hôpital si on a mal à la ⬜⬜⬜⬜ .

TRANSLATION

1. *He hurt his back carrying that heavy box.*
2. *She has too many bracelets on her wrist.*
3. *We wear our wedding ring on our ring finger.*
4. *The kidneys filter toxins from the body.*
5. *She has a small bladder. She always has to go to the bathroom.*
6. *Don't put your elbows on the table.*
7. *I often have calf cramps.*
8. *His shoulder is sore since his tennis match.*
9. *She always has polish on her nails.*
10. *You have to go to the hospital if you have chest pain.*

LES VERBES DE LA CUISINE
COOKING VERBS

15

Ajouter v | *To add*
Assaisonner v | *To season*
Battre v | *To whisk*
Chauffer v | *To heat*
Couper en dés v | *To dice*
Couper en lamelles v | *To slice*
Couper v | *To cut*
Cuire à la vapeur v | *To steam*
Cuire au four v | *To bake*
Cuisiner v | *To cook*
Déguster v | *To enjoy*
Écraser v | *To crush*
Égoutter v | *To drain*
Enfourner v | *To put in the oven*
Éplucher v | *To peel*
Faire bouillir v | *To boil*
Faire cuire v | *To cook*
Faire fondre v | *To melt*
Faire revenir v | *To brown*
Faire sauter v | *To saute*
Fouetter v | *To whisk*
Frire v | *To fry*

Goûter v | *To taste*
Hacher v | *To chop*
Incorporer v | *To stir in*
Mariner v | *To marinate*
Mélanger v | *To blend – To mix*
Mesurer v | *To measure*
Mijoter v | *To simmer*
Mixer v | *To mix*
Peser v | *To weigh*
Porter à ébullition v | *To bring to a boil*
Préchauffer v | *To preheat*
Préparer v | *To prepare*
Râper v | *To grate*
Réduire v | *To reduce*
Remplir v | *To fill*
Remuer v | *To blend – To mix*
Rincer v | *To rinse*
Rôtir v | *To roast*
Servir v | *To serve*
Trancher v | *To slice*
Tremper v | *To soak*
Verser v | *To pour*

Ajoutez **les verbes** à la recette.
Add the verbs to the recipe.

Nouilles au beurre de cacahuètes
Noodles with peanut butter sauce

ajoutez – ajoutez – ajoutez – bouillir – cuire – dégustez – égouttez – fouettez –
goûtez – hachez – mélangez – remplissez – revenir – sauter – servez

1. _____ une casserole d'eau. Faites _____ l'eau

   et _____ les nouilles. Faites _____ les nouilles

   selon les instructions du paquet.

ajoutez – ajoutez – ajoutez – bouillir – cuire – dégustez – égouttez – fouettez – goûtez – hachez – mélangez – remplissez – revenir – sauter – servez

2. ⬚⬚⬚⬚⬚⬚⬚⬚ l'ail et ajoutez-le dans une poêle avec une cuillère à soupe d'huile. Faites ⬚⬚⬚⬚⬚⬚⬚⬚ à feu doux pendant environ deux minutes ou jusqu'à ce que l'ail soit doré. ⬚⬚⬚⬚⬚⬚⬚⬚ le gingembre et faites ⬚⬚⬚⬚⬚⬚⬚⬚ une minute de plus.

3. ⬚⬚⬚⬚⬚⬚⬚⬚ tous les ingrédients restants de la sauce et ⬚⬚⬚⬚⬚⬚⬚⬚ pour atteindre la consistance souhaitée.

4. ⬚⬚⬚⬚⬚⬚⬚⬚ et ajoutez plus de sauce soja ou de sauce piquante selon vos goûts.

5. ⬚⬚⬚⬚⬚⬚⬚⬚ les nouilles et ajoutez plus ou moins la moitié de la sauce aux nouilles cuites et ⬚⬚⬚⬚⬚⬚⬚⬚ .

6. ⬚⬚⬚⬚⬚⬚⬚⬚ avec des cacahuètes, des brocolis, des carottes, des oignons verts et ⬚⬚⬚⬚⬚⬚⬚⬚ !

TRANSLATION

1. *Fill a pot with water. Boil the water and add the noodles. Cook the noodles according to package directions.*

2. *Chop the garlic and add it to a pan with a tablespoon of oil. Sauté over low heat for about two minutes or until the garlic is golden brown. Add the ginger and fry for another minute.*

3. *Add all remaining sauce ingredients and whisk to reach desired consistency.*

4. *Taste and add more soy sauce or hot sauce if needed.*

5. *Drain the noodles and add about half of the sauce to the cooked noodles and mix.*

6. *Serve with peanuts, broccoli, carrots, green onions and enjoy!*

QUELLE EST LA BONNE ORTHOGRAPHE ?

16

WHAT IS THE RIGHT SPELLING?

 Choisissez **la bonne orthographe** parmi les deux mots donnés.
Choose the right spelling from the two spellings given.

1. **diplomes – diplômes** – Les élèves ont reçu leurs   à la fin de l'année scolaire.

2. **vacance – vacances** – Qu'est-ce que tu as de prévu en   ?

3. **Apparemment – Apparement** –   , il vient de demander le divorce.

4. **circonstances – circonstences** – Je ne connais pas les   de l'accident.

5. **consience – conscience** – Il a mauvaise   après ce qu'il a dit.

6. **recommander – recommender** – Est-ce que tu peux me   un bon restaurant ?

7. **immédiate – imédiate** – J'ai besoin d'une réponse   .

8. **lavande – lavende** – On a pris des photos devant ce champ de   .

9. **poireaux – porreaux** – Est-ce que tu as une bonne recette de soupe aux   ?

10. **ognions – oignons** – Les   me font toujours pleurer.

11. **documantaire – documentaire** – Ce   est un succès.

12. **passport – passeport** – N'oublie pas de prendre ton   .

13. **applaudissements – aplaudissements** – Elle a reçu beaucoup d'   après son concert.

14. **boullir – bouillir** – Faites   l'eau avant d'y mettre les pâtes.

15. **papillons – pappillons** – Il y a des   sur les fleurs.

VOCABULARY

Un – Une élève n | *A student*

Recevoir v | *To receive*

Un diplôme nm | *A diploma*

Une année scolaire nf | *A school year*

Les vacances nf | *Vacation*

Apparemment adv | *Apparently*

Demander v | *To ask – To fill*

Un divorce nm | *A divorce*

Une circonstance nf | *A circumstance*

Un accident nm | *An accident*

Avoir mauvaise conscience | *To have a guilty conscience*

Recommander v | *To recommend*

Un bon restaurant | *A good restaurant*

Une réponse nf | *A response*

Immédiat – Immédiate adj | *Immediate*

Prendre des photos | *To take photos*

Un champ de lavande nm | *A lavender field*

Une bonne recette | *A good recipe*

Une soupe aux poireaux nf | *A leek soup*

Un oignon nm | *An onion*

Pleurer v | *To cry*

Un documentaire nm | *A documentary*

Un succès nm | *A success*

Un passeport nm | *A passport*

Des applaudissements nm | *Applause*

Un concert nm | *A concert*

Bouillir v | *To boil*

De l'eau nf | *Water*

Des pâtes nf | *Pasta*

Un papillon nm | *A butterfly*

Une fleur nf | *A flower*

TRANSLATION

1. *The students received their diplomas at the end of the school year.*
2. *What do you have planned for vacation?*
3. *Apparently he just filed for divorce.*
4. *I don't know the circumstances of the accident.*
5. *He has a guilty conscience after what he said.*
6. *Can you recommend a good restaurant for me?*

7. *I need an immediate response.*
8. *We took photos in front of this lavender field.*
9. *Do you have a good recipe for leek soup?*
10. *Onions always make me cry.*
11. *This documentary is a success.*
12. *Don't forget to take your passport.*
13. *She received a lot of applause after her concert.*
14. *Boil the water before adding the pasta.*
15. *There are butterflies on the flowers.*

LES ADJECTIFS ET LEURS CONTRAIRES

17

ADJECTIVES AND THEIR OPPOSITES

AUDIO 17.1 🔊

Here are some common French adjectives and their opposites. Each adjective is given as masculine and feminine, unless the adjective doesn't change with gender.

Bas – Basse | *Low*
Beau – Belle | *Beautiful*
Bon – Bonne | *Good*
Bon marché | *Cheap*
Content – Contente | *Happy*
Courageux – Courageuse | *Brave*
Court – Courte | *Short*
Facile | *Easy*
Faible | *Weak*
Fidèle | *Faithful*
Froid – Froide | *Cold*
Gentil – Gentille | *Kind*
Heureux – Heureuse | *Happy*
Jeune | *Young*
Léger – Légère | *Light*
Lent – Lente | *Slow*
Libre | *Free*
Mou – Molle | *Soft*
Naturel – Naturelle | *Natural*
Nouveau – Nouvelle | *New*
Organisé – Organisée | *Organized*
Ouvert – Ouverte | *Open*
Petit – Petite | *Short*
Poli – Polie | *Polite*
Propre | *Clean*
Riche | *Rich*
Sain – Saine | *Healthy*
Sec – Sèche | *Dry*

Haut – Haute | *High*
Laid – Laide | *Ugly*
Mauvais – Mauvaise | *Bad*
Cher – Chère | *Expensive*
Mécontent – Mécontente | *Unhappy*
Lâche | *Coward*
Long – Longue | *Long*
Difficile | *Difficult*
Fort – Forte | *Strong*
Infidèle | *Unfaithful*
Chaud – Chaude | *Hot*
Méchant – Méchante | *Mean*
Triste | *Sad*
Vieux – Vieille | *Old*
Lourd – Lourde | *Heavy*
Rapide | *Fast*
Occupé – Occupée | *Busy*
Dur – Dure | *Hard*
Artificiel – Artificielle | *Artificial*
Ancien – Ancienne | *Old*
Désorganisé – Désorganisée | *Disorganized*
Fermé – Fermée | *Closed*
Grand – Grande | *Tall*
Impoli – Impolie | *Rude*
Sale | *Dirty*
Pauvre | *Poor*
Malade | *Sick*
Humide | *Wet*

Silencieux – Silencieuse | *Silent*
Sucré – Sucrée | *Sweet*
Sympathique | *Friendly*
Utile | *Useful*
Vide | *Empty*

Bavard – Bavarde | *Talkative*
Salé – Salée | *Salty*
Antipathique | *Unfriendly*
Inutile | *Useless*
Plein – Pleine | *Full*

AUDIO 17.2 ◀)

 Trouvez **l'adjectif** et réécrivez la phrase en remplaçant l'adjectif par **son contraire**.
Find the adjective and rewrite the sentence, replacing the adjective with its opposite.

1. Ce gâteau est tellement bon !

2. Fais attention, l'eau du bain est très chaude.

3. Son mari a toujours été fidèle.

4. Le magasin est déjà ouvert.

5. Ce puzzle est trop difficile pour moi.

6. Il a toujours été gentil avec mes parents.

7. C'est le pont le plus long du pays.

8. Tous les ingrédients de ce produit sont artificiels.

9. Est-ce que tu es occupé ce samedi ?

10. Sa maison est toujours organisée.

11. Je pense que cette chemise est sale.

12. L'herbe était humide ce matin.

13. Le plat est assez salé pour moi.

14. Cet outil est utile pour ce projet.

15. Le réservoir de ma voiture est plein.

TRANSLATION

1. *This cake is so good!*
2. *Be careful, the bath water is very hot.*
3. *Her husband has always been faithful.*
4. *The store is already open.*
5. *This puzzle is too difficult for me.*
6. *He was always kind to my parents.*
7. *It is the longest bridge in the country.*
8. *All ingredients in this product are artificial.*
9. *Are you busy this Saturday?*
10. *Her house is always organized.*
11. *I think this shirt is dirty.*
12. *The grass was wet this morning.*
13. *The dish is salty enough for me.*
14. *This tool is useful for this project.*
15. *My car's gas tank is full.*

LES ÉLÉMENTS DE LA CUISINE
KITCHEN ELEMENTS

18

Un (four à) micro-ondes nm | *A microwave oven*
Une bouilloire nf | *A kettle*
Une cafetière nf | *A coffee machine*
Un congélateur nm | *A freezer*
Une cuisinière à gaz nf | *A gas stove*
Un égouttoir nm | *A dish rack*
Un évier nm | *A sink*
Un four nm | *An oven*
Un grille-pain nm | *A toaster*
Un îlot de cuisine nm | *A kitchen island*
Un lave-vaisselle nm | *A dishwasher*
Un mixeur nm | *A blender*
Une poubelle nf | *A trash bin*
Un réfrigérateur nm | *A refrigerator*
Un robinet nm | *A faucet*
Une table de cuisine nf | *A kitchen table*
Une théière nf | *A teapot*

Une balance nf | *A scale*
Une casserole nf | *A pot*
Des ciseaux nm | *Scissors*
Un couteau nm | *A knife*
Un couteau à pain nm | *A bread knife*
Une cuillère en bois nf | *A woodspoon*
Un éplucheur nm | *A peeler*
Une essoreuse à salade nf | *A salad spinner*
Un fouet nm | *A whisk*
Une louche nf | *A ladle*
Une manique nf | *An oven mit*
Un ouvre-boîtes nm | *A can opener*
Une passoire nf | *A strainer*
Une planche à découper nf | *A cutting board*
Une poêle nf | *A pan – A skillet*
Une spatule nf | *A spatula*

La vaisselle nf | *Dishes*
Une assiette nf | *A plate*
Un bol nm | *A bowl*
Une tasse nf | *A cup*
Un verre nm | *A glass*
Un verre à vin nm | *A wine glass*

Les couverts nm | *Cutlery – Silverware*
Un couteau nm | *A knife*
Une cuillère nf | *A spoon*
Une cuillère à café nf | *A teaspoon*
Une cuillère à soupe nf | *A tablespoon*
Une fourchette nf | *A fork*

Une nappe nf | *A tablecloth*
Un poivrier nm | *A pepper shaker*
Une salière nf | *A saltshaker*
Une serviette nf | *A napkin*

AUDIO 18.2 🔊

 Ajoutez **le bon mot** à chaque phrase en utilisant la liste ci-dessus.
Add the correct word to each sentence using the list above.

1. Pour faire du café, j'utilise la _____.

2. Pour cuire un gâteau, j'utilise le _____.

3. Pour nettoyer la vaisselle, j'utilise le _____.

4. Pour conserver les aliments, je les mets au _____.

5. Pour congeler mes plats, je les mets au _____.

6. Pour faire du thé, j'utilise la _____.

7. Pour griller du pain, j'utilise le _____.

8. Pour réchauffer un plat, j'utilise un _____.

9. Pour éplucher les carottes, j'utilise un _____.

10. Pour ouvrir une boîte de conserve, j'utilise un _____.

Question personnelle – Avant de manger votre dîner, qu'est-ce que vous mettez sur la table ?

Personal question – Before eating your dinner, what do you put on the table?

TRANSLATION

1. *To make coffee, I use the coffee maker.*

2. *To bake a cake, I use the oven.*

3. *To clean dishes, I use the dishwasher.*

4. *To preserve food, I put it in the refrigerator.*

5. *To freeze my meals, I put them in the freezer.*

6. *To make tea, I use the teapot.*

7. *To toast bread, I use the toaster.*

8. *To reheat a dish, I use a microwave.*

9. *To peel carrots, I use a peeler.*

10. *To open a can, I use a can opener.*

VRAI OU FAUX
TRUE OR FALSE

19

 Est-ce que ces phrases sont vraies ou fausses pour vous ? Écrivez **Vrai (V)** ou **Faux (F)** devant chaque phrase. Le vocabulaire est listé après l'exercice.
Are these sentences true or false for you? Write Vrai (V) or Faux (F) in front of each sentence. The vocabulary is listed after the exercise.

1.   Je mesure plus d'un mètre soixante.

2.   Je prends toujours un petit déjeuner.

3.   Je parle deux langues couramment.

4.   Je préfère regarder un film plutôt qu'une série télévisée.

5.   Je fais toujours mon ménage le dimanche.

6.   Je travaille à domicile.

7.   Je suis abonné(e) à un journal ou un magazine.

8.   Je porte des lunettes.

9.   Je mange des légumes à chaque repas.

10.   Je lis au moins un livre par mois.

11.   J'aime manger au restaurant de temps en temps.

12.   Je préfère me lever tard.

13.   Je suis introverti(e) plutôt qu'extraverti(e).

14.   Je préfère les vacances à la montagne plutôt qu'à la plage.

15.   Je conduis ma voiture tous les jours.

16.   Je vais souvent au cinéma pour voir un film.

17.   Je fais mes courses en ligne plutôt qu'en magasin.

18.   J'étudie le français tous les jours.

19.   J'aime recevoir mes amis chez moi.

20.   Je sais jouer de la guitare.

AUDIO 19.2 ◄)))

VOCABULARY

Mesurer v | *To measure (To be over – under)*
Un mètre nm | *A meter*
Prendre v | *To have*
Un petit déjeuner nm | *A breakfast*
Parler v | *To speak*
Une langue nf | *A language*
Couramment adv | *Fluently*
Préférer v | *To prefer*
Regarder v | *To watch*
Un film nm | *A movie*
Une série télévisée nf | *A TV Series*
Faire le ménage | *To do the cleaning*
Le dimanche nm | *Sunday*
Travailler v | *To work*
Un domicile nm | *From home*
Être abonné(e) v | *To be subscribed*
Un journal nm | *A newspaper*
Un magazine nm | *A magazine*
Porter v | *To wear*
Des lunettes nf | *Glasses*
Manger v | *To eat*
Des légumes nm | *Vegetables*
Un repas nm | *A meal*
Lire v | *To read*
Un livre nm | *A book*
Un mois nm | *A month*

Aimer v | *To like – To love*
Manger v | *To eat*
Un restaurant nm | *A restaurant*
Se lever v | *To get up*
Tard adv | *Late*
Introverti(e) adj | *Introverted*
Extraverti(e) adj | *Extroverted*
Les vacances nf | *Vacations*
La montagne nf | *The mountain*
La plage nf | *The beach*
Conduire v | *To drive*
Une voiture nf | *A car*
Aller v | *To go*
Le cinéma nm | *The theater*
Voir v | *To see*
Faire les courses | *To shop*
En ligne adv | *Online*
Un magasin nm | *A shop*
Étudier v | *To study*
Le français nm | *French*
Recevoir v | *To entertain*
Un ami – Une amie n | *A friend*
Savoir v | *To know*
Jouer v | *To play*
Une guitare nf | *A guitar*

TRANSLATION

1. *I'm over one metre sixty.*
2. *I always have breakfast.*
3. *I speak two languages fluently.*
4. *I prefer to watch a movie rather than a TV series.*

5. *I always do my cleaning on Sunday.*

6. *I work from home.*

7. *I subscribe to a newspaper or magazine.*

8. *I wear glasses.*

9. *I eat vegetables with every meal.*

10. *I read at least one book a month.*

11. *I like to eat out from time to time.*

12. *I prefer to get up late.*

13. *I am introverted rather than extroverted.*

14. *I prefer vacations in the mountains rather than at the beach.*

15. *I drive my car every day.*

16. *I often go to the cinema to see a film.*

17. *I shop online rather than in store.*

18. *I study French every day.*

19. *I like to entertain my friends at my house.*

20. *I know how to play guitar.*

LA JOURNÉE DE DANY
DANY'S DAY

20

AUDIO 20.1 ◄))

Bon – Bonne adj | *Good*
Chargé – Chargée adj | *Busy*
Content – Contente adj | *Happy*
Dernier – Dernière adj | *Last*
En panne adj | *Broken*
Ennuyant – Ennuyante adj | *Boring*
Éprouvant – Éprouvante adj | *Challenging*
Fatigué – Fatiguée adj | *Tired*

Frustré – Frustrée adj | *Frustrated*
Impatient – Impatiente adj | *Impatient*
Interminable adj | *Endless*
Lent – Lente adj | *Slow*
Long – Longue adj | *Long*
Occupé – Occupée adj | *Busy*
Stressant – Stressante adj | *Stressful*

AUDIO 20.2 ◄))

Ajoutez **le bon adjectif** de la liste ci-dessus au texte. N'oubliez pas de choisir **le masculin** ou **le féminin**.
Add the correct adjective from the list above to the text. Don't forget to choose masculine or feminine.

Dany a commencé la journée avec un   petit déjeuner. Il a une journée   au bureau aujourd'hui avec une réunion et une conférence. La réunion va sûrement être   car il y a beaucoup de problèmes à régler. La conférence, elle, va certainement être   .

Quand Dany arrive au bureau, il se sent tout de suite   . Son ordinateur est   et personne ne peut venir le réparer. Toute l'équipe informatique est   ce matin. Il peut utiliser son ordinateur portable mais il est très   . Cela va lui prendre un temps   de préparer sa réunion. Il est 10 heures et Dany est déjà   . La journée va être   .

Après sa réunion, Dany va prendre son déjeuner. La réunion a été   . Il est   qu'elle soit finie ! À 14 heures, il doit aller à une conférence pour parler du   trimestre de l'année. Il est   de rentrer chez lui.

TRANSLATION

Dany started the day with a good breakfast. He has a busy day at the office today with a meeting and a conference. The meeting is sure to be stressful because there are a lot of issues to resolve. The conference is definitely going to be boring.

When Dany arrives at the office, he immediately feels frustrated. His computer is broken and no one can come and fix it. The entire IT team is busy this morning. He can use his laptop but it is very slow. It's going to take him forever to prepare for his meeting. It's 10 o'clock and Dany is already tired. The day is going to be long.

After his meeting, Dany goes to have lunch. The meeting was challenging. He's glad it's finished! At 2 p.m. he has to go to a conference to talk about the last quarter of the year. He can't wait to get home.

LES ANAGRAMMES

ANAGRAMS

21

What is an anagram?

An anagram is a word formed by rearranging the letters of another word.

Example: cas = sac

AUDIO 21.1 ◀ঠ)

Trouvez **le mot manquant** en vous basant sur le premier mot. La liste des mots est traduite après cet exercice.
Find the missing word based on the first word. The list of words is translated after this exercise.

1. **niche** – Mon _____ joue dans le jardin avec sa balle.

2. **port** – J'ai _____ de pommes de terre dans mon assiette.

3. **mon** – Est-ce que tu peux épeler ton _____ ?

4. **ami** – On a réservé un hôtel pour le mois de _____ .

5. **soif** – Mes parents ont visité cette ville plusieurs _____ quand ils étaient jeunes.

6. **ride** – Qu'est-ce que tu veux _____ ?

7. **obéir** – Ce n'est pas bon de _____ trop d'alcool.

8. **coupe** – Il s'est coupé le _____ en travaillant dans le jardin.

9. **neige** – C'est une idée de _____ !

10. **charme** – Fais attention à la _____ .

11. **rose** – Il faut _____ faire ce qu'on veut dans la vie.

12. **stop** – On a beaucoup de plantes en _____ sur notre terrasse.

13. **suer** – Les _____ de la capitale sont bondées.

14. **rois** – Qu'est-ce que tu fais ce _____ ?

15. **lime** – Ce _____ est délicieux !

TRANSLATED WORDS

Une niche nf | *A niche*
Un port nm | *A port*
Mon adj | *My*
Un ami nm | *A friend*
La soif nf | *Thirst*
Une ride nf | *A wrinkle*
Obéir v | *To obey*
Une coupe nf | *A cut*

La neige nf | *Snow*
Le charme nm | *Charm*
Une rose nf | *A rose*
Un stop nm | *A stop*
Suer v | *To sweat*
Les rois nm | *Kings*
Une lime nf | *A file*

TRANSLATION

1. *My dog plays in the garden with his ball.*

2. *I have too many potatoes on my plate.*

3. *Can you spell your name?*

4. *We booked a hotel for the month of May.*

5. *My parents visited this city several times when they were young.*

6. *What do you mean ?*

7. *It's not good to drink too much alcohol.*

8. *He cut his thumb while working in the garden.*

9. *It's a genius idea!*

10. *Be careful when walking.*

11. *You have to dare to do what you want in life.*

12. *We have a lot of potted plants on our terrace.*

13. *The streets of the capital are crowded.*

14. *What are you doing tonight?*

15. *This honey is delicious!*

LES QUANTITÉS
QUANTITIES

AUDIO 22.1 ◀ᵢ))

Mesurer v | *To measure*
Peser v | *To weigh*

Une boîte de nf | *A box of – A can of*
Une bouteille de nf | *A bottle of*
Une canette de nf | *A can of*
Une cuillère à café de nf | *A teaspoon of*
Une cuillère à soupe de nf | *A tablespoon of*
Une livre de nf | *A pound of*
Un morceau de nm | *A piece of*

Un paquet de nm | *A pack of – A bag of*
Un pot de nm | *A jar of*
Une tablette de nf | *A bar of*
Une tasse de nf | *A cup of*
Une tranche de nf | *A slice of*
Un verre de nm | *A glass of*

Un milligramme nm | *A milligram*
Un gramme nm | *A gram*
Un kilo nm | *A kilo*
Une tonne nf | *A ton*
Un millilitre nm | *A milliliter*
Un litre nm | *A liter*

AUDIO 22.2 ◀ᵢ))

 Ajoutez une des **quantités** de la liste ci-dessus à chaque phrase.
Add one of the quantities from the list above to each sentence.

1. Ce _____ chips est déjà ouvert.

2. Le _____ confiture est sur la table si tu en veux.

3. Je mange deux _____ pain tous les matins.

4. On a mangé une _____ chocolat devant la télévision.

5. Est-ce que tu veux un _____ gâteau ?

6. Il boit une _____ eau pétillante avec son dîner.

7. La recette dit d'ajouter deux _____ à café de sucre.

8. 1000 grammes = 1

9. 1000 kilos = 1

10. 1000 millilitres = 1

TRANSLATION

1. *This bag of chips is already opened.*
2. *The jar of jam is on the table if you want some.*
3. *I eat two slices of bread every morning.*
4. *We ate a chocolate bar in front of the television.*
5. *Do you want a piece of cake?*
6. *He drinks a can/bottle of sparkling water with his dinner.*
7. *The recipe says to add two teaspoons of sugar.*
8. *1000 grams = 1 kilo*
9. *1000 kilos = 1 ton*
10. *1000 milliliters = 1 liter*

LA ROUTINE DU MATIN ET DU SOIR
MORNING AND NIGHT ROUTINE

23

AUDIO 23.1 ◀))

S'habiller v | *To get dressed*
Se déshabiller v | *To get undressed*
Se brosser les cheveux | *To brush one's hair*
Se démaquiller v | *To remove makeup*
S'épiler v | *To pluck – To wax*
Se laver v | *To wash yourself*
Se maquiller v | *To put on makeup*
Prendre une douche | *To take a shower*
Prendre un bain | *To take a bath*
Sentir bon | *To smell good*

Se brosser les dents | *To brush one's teeth*
Une brosse à dents nf | *A toothbrush*
Une brosse à dents électrique nf | *An electric toothbrush*
Utiliser du fil dentaire | *To floss*
Du bain de bouche nm | *Mouthwash*
Du dentifrice nm | *Toothpaste*
Du fil dentaire nm | *Floss*

Se raser v | *To shave*
Un rasoir nm | *A razor*

Se laver les cheveux | *To wash your hair*
L'après-shampoing nm | *Conditioner*
Le déodorant nm | *Deodorant*
Le gel douche nm | *Shower gel*
Le savon nm | *Soap*
Le shampoing nm | *Shampoo*

AUDIO 23.2 ◀))

 Ajoutez **le bon mot** ou **groupe de mots** à chaque phrase.
Add the correct word or group of words to each sentence.

> après-shampoing – bain – brosse à dents électrique – déodorant – fil dentaire –
> m'habille – me brosse – me démaquille – me déshabille – me maquille – rasoir –
> savon – se laver – se rasent – sens bon

1. Pour rester propre, c'est important de _____ chaque jour.

2. Le matin, je _____ avant de sortir de ma chambre.

3. Je _____ les cheveux et les dents.

4. Le soir, j'aime prendre un _____ pour me détendre.

après-shampoing – bain – brosse à dents électrique – déodorant – fil dentaire – m'habille – me brosse – me démaquille – me déshabille – me maquille – rasoir – savon – se laver – se rasent – sens bon

5. Après mon bain, je mets du _____ pour ne pas sentir la transpiration.

6. Quand je rentre chez moi, je _____ et je me mets en pyjama.

7. Avant de me coucher, je _____ avec un produit doux.

8. Après le shampoing, j'utilise de _____ pour démêler mes cheveux.

9. Beaucoup d'hommes _____ avant d'aller au bureau.

10. Je préfère me laver avec du _____ plutôt qu'avec du gel douche.

11. Je _____ presque tous les jours.

12. C'est bien d'utiliser du _____ avant de se laver les dents.

13. Ma _____ n'a plus de batterie.

14. Est-ce que tu as vu mon _____ ?

15. Je _____ après un bain moussant.

TRANSLATION

1. *To stay clean, it's important to wash every day.*
2. *In the morning, I get dressed before leaving my room.*
3. *I brush my hair and my teeth.*
4. *In the evening, I like to take a bath to relax.*
5. *After my bath, I put on deodorant so I don't smell like sweat.*
6. *When I get home, I undress and change into my pajamas.*
7. *Before going to bed, I remove my makeup with a gentle product.*
8. *After shampooing, I use conditioner to detangle my hair.*
9. *Many men shave before going to the office.*
10. *I prefer to wash with soap rather than shower gel.*
11. *I wear makeup almost every day.*
12. *It's good to floss before brushing your teeth.*
13. *My electric toothbrush has run out of battery.*
14. *Have you seen my razor?*
15. *I smell good after a bubble bath.*

LE JARDIN
THE GARDEN

24

Un arbre nm | *A tree*
Un buisson nm | *A bush*
Une clôture nf | *A fence*
Un feu nm | *A fire pit*
Une fleur nf | *A flower*
Une haie nf | *A hedge*

Un jardin nm | *A garden*
Les mauvaises herbes nf | *Weeds*
Une tondeuse nf | *A lawn mower*
Une pelouse nf | *A lawn*
Un potager nm | *A vegetable garden*

Une balançoire nf | *A swing*
Une chaise d'extérieur nf | *An outdoor chair*
Une chaise longue nf | *A lounge chair*

Un hamac nm | *A hammock*
Un parasol nm | *An umbrella*
Une table d'extérieur nf | *An outdoor table*

Arroser v | *To water*
Creuser v | *To dig*
Cueillir v | *To pick*
Cultiver v | *To cultivate*
Faire pousser v | *To grow*
Fleurir v | *To blossom*
Jardiner v | *To garden*

Planter v | *To plant*
Pousser v | *To grow*
Récolter v | *To harvest*
Semer v | *To seed*
Tailler v | *To trim*
Tondre v | *To mow*

Arracher les mauvaises herbes | *To pull up weeds*
Arroser les plantes | *To water the plant*
Entretenir le jardin | *To maintain the garden*
Faire du compost | *To compost*

Ramasser les feuilles | *To pick up leaves*
S'occuper du jardin | *To take care of the yard*
Tailler les haies | *To trim the hedges*
Tondre la pelouse | *To mow the lawn*

 Choisissez entre **les deux mots** pour chaque phrase.
Choose between the two words for each sentence.

1. **pousser – tailler** – Le fertilisant aide à faire   les légumes.

2. **chaise longue – chaise d'extérieur** – Ma mère adore s'allonger sur cette   .

3. **arroser – cultiver** – Il faut   les plantes quand il fait trop chaud.

4. **tondeuse – clôture** – Mon jardin est fermé par une   .

5. **faire pousser – jardiner** – J'adore   quand j'ai du temps libre.

6. **fleurs – potagers** – Au printemps, certaines   commencent à éclore.

7. **a récolté – a semé** – On   les graines il y a un mois mais rien ne pousse.

8. **hamac – parasol** – On a acheté   pour avoir de l'ombre quand on est assis dehors.

9. **creuser – récolter** – Il est temps de   les pommes avant que les oiseaux ne les mangent.

10. **jardin – potager** – J'ai commencé un   avec des carottes, des courgettes et des pommes de terre.

11. **récolte – tond** – Le voisin   sa pelouse tous les samedis matin.

12. **hamac – balançoire** – Quand j'aurai un jardin, j'aurai un   pour faire des siestes.

13. **arrose – cultive** – Le fermier   ce champ depuis des années.

14. **serre – haie** – La   permet de faire pousser des fleurs toute l'année.

15. **taille – tond** – Le jardinier   les buissons.

TRANSLATION

1. *Fertilizer helps vegetables grow.*
2. *My mother loves lying on this lounge chair.*
3. *Plants should be watered when it is too hot.*
4. *My garden is closed in by a fence.*
5. *I love gardening when I have free time.*
6. *In spring, some flowers begin to bloom.*
7. *We sowed the seeds a month ago but nothing is growing.*
8. *We bought an umbrella to provide shade when sitting outside.*
9. *It's time to harvest the apples before the birds eat them.*

10. *I started a vegetable garden with carrots, zucchini and potatoes.*

11. *The neighbor mows his lawn every Saturday morning.*

12. *When I have a garden, I will have a hammock for naps.*

13. *The farmer has been cultivating this field for years.*

14. *The greenhouse allows you to grow flowers all year round.*

15. *The gardener prunes the bushes.*

J'AIME – JE N'AIME PAS
I LIKE – I DON'T LIKE

 Décrivez ce que **vous aimez** ou **n'aimez pas** et ce que **vous aimez** ou **n'aimez pas faire**. Il y a deux structures possibles.
Describe what you like or don't like and what you like or don't like to do.
Two possible structures

AUDIO 25.1 🔊

Followed by a noun:

J'aime <u>le chocolat</u>. *I like chocolate.*
Je n'aime pas <u>le chocolat</u>. *I do not like chocolate.*

Followed by an infinitive verb:

J'aime <u>nettoyer</u>. *I like to clean.*
Je n'aime pas <u>nettoyer</u>. *I don't like cleaning.*

AUDIO 25.2 🔊

1. J'aime

2. J'aime

3. J'aime

4. J'aime

5. J'aime

6. Je n'aime pas

7. Je n'aime pas

8. Je n'aime pas

9. Je n'aime pas

10. Je n'aime pas

LES ARBRES ET LES FRUITS
TREES AND FRUITS

26

Les arbres fruitiers – *Fruit trees*

Un abricotier nm | *An apricot tree*
Un avocatier nm | *An avocado tree*
Un bananier nm | *A banana tree*
Un cerisier nm | *A cherry tree*
Un citronnier nm | *A lemon tree*
Un cocotier nm | *A coconut tree*
Un figuier nm | *A fig tree*
Un grenadier nm | *A pomegranate tree*
Un kaki nm | *A persimmon tree*
Un litchi nm | *A lychee tree*
Un manguier nm | *A mango tree*
Un olivier nm | *An olive tree*
Un oranger nm | *An orange tree*
Un papayer nm | *A papaya tree*
Un pêcher nm | *A peach tree*
Un poirier nm | *A pear tree*
Un pommier nm | *An apple tree*
Un prunier nm | *A plum tree*

Un abricot nm | *An apricot*
Un avocat nm | *An avocado*
Une banane nf | *A banana*
Une cerise nf | *A cherry*
Un citron nm | *A lemon*
Une noix de coco nf | *A coconut*
Une figue nf | *A fig*
Une grenade nf | *A pomegranate*
Un kaki nm | *A persimmon*
Un litchi nm | *A lychee*
Une mangue nf | *A mango*
Une olive nf | *An olive*
Une orange nf | *An orange*
Une papaye nf | *A papaya*
Une pêche nf | *A peach*
Une poire nf | *A pear*
Une pomme nf | *An apple*
Une prune nf | *A plum*

Les arbustres – *Bushes and Plants*

Un cassissier nm | *A blackcurrant bush*
Un fraisier nm | *A strawberry plant*
Un framboisier nm | *A raspberry bush*
Un groseillier nm | *A currant bush*
Un mûrier nm | *A mulberry bush*
Un myrtillier nm | *A blueberry bush*

Un cassis nm | *A blackcurrant*
Une fraise nf | *A strawberry*
Une framboise nf | *A raspberry*
Une groseille nf | *A currant*
Une mûre nf | *A mulberry*
Une myrtille nf | *A blueberry*

Autre – *Other*

Un érable nm | *A maple tree*

Le sirop d'érable nm | *Maple syrup*

> 📝 Ajoutez **le bon fruit ou sirop** à chaque phrase.
> *Add the right fruit or syrup to each sentence.*

1. Le _____ vient de l'érable.

2. Les _____ poussent sur le citronnier.

3. Les _____ poussent sur le cerisier.

4. Les _____ poussent sur le pommier.

5. Les _____ poussent sur le fraisier.

6. Les _____ poussent sur l'avocatier.

7. Les _____ poussent sur l'olivier.

8. Les _____ poussent sur l'oranger.

9. Les _____ poussent sur le prunier.

10. Les _____ poussent sur le bananier.

11. Les _____ poussent sur le manguier.

12. Les _____ poussent sur le framboisier.

TRANSLATION

1. *Maple syrup comes from maple trees.*
2. *Lemons grow on the lemon tree.*
3. *Cherries grow on the cherry tree.*
4. *Apples grow on the apple tree.*
5. *Strawberries grow on the strawberry bush.*
6. *Avocados grow on the avocado tree.*
7. *Olives grow on the olive tree.*
8. *Oranges grow on the orange tree.*
9. *Plums grow on the plum tree.*
10. *Bananas grow on the banana tree.*
11. *Mangoes grow on the mango tree.*
12. *Raspberries grow on the raspberry bush.*

Below you can find common words related to studying. Read and study the vocabulary before filling up the crossword or challenge yourself and try directly the crossword.

AUDIO 27.1 ◀))

Apprendre v | *To learn*
Une bibliothèque nf | *A library*
Une bibliothèque universitaire nf |
A university library
Une bourse d'études nf | *A scholarship*
Un cahier nm | *A notebook*
La compréhension nf | *Comprehension*
Comprendre v | *To learn*
Une conférence nf | *A lecture*
Un cours nm | *A course*
Un devoir nm | *Homework*
Un dictionnaire nm | *A dictionary*
Un diplôme nm | *A diploma*
Une dissertation nf | *An essay*
Une école nf | *A school*
Les études nf | *Studies*
Un étudiant – Une étudiante n | *A student*
Étudier v | *To study*
Une évaluation nf | *An assessment*
Un examen nm | *An exam*
Une exception nf | *An exception*
Un exercice nm | *An exercise*
Une faculté nf | *A faculty*
Une formation nf | *Training*
La grammaire nf | *Grammar*
Un instituteur – Une institutrice n |
A primary school teacher
Une langue nf | *A language*

Une leçon nf | *A lesson*
La lecture nf | *Reading*
Un manuel nm | *A textbook*
Une matière nf | *A subject*
Un mémoire nm | *A thesis*
Une méthode nf | *A method*
Un niveau nm | *A level*
Une note nf | *A grade*
Un professeur – Une professeure n | *A teacher*
Des progrès nm | *Progress*
Une question nf | *A question*
Une recherche nf | *Research*
Une règle nf | *A rule*
Une réponse nf | *An answer*
Une révision nf | *A review*
Une salle de classe nf | *A classroom*
Un stage nm | *An internship*
Un sujet nm | *A topic*
Un tableau nm | *A blackboard/whiteboard*
Une traduction nf | *A translation*
Une université nf | *A university*
Le vocabulaire nm | *Vocabulary*

Ajoutez la traduction de chaque mot dans **les cases numérotées**. Pour les noms, ajoutez seulement le nom et pas l'article.

Add the translation of each word in the numbered boxes. For nouns, add only the noun and not the article.

ACROSS

1. exercise
2. student (masculine)
3. translation
4. language

5. rule
6. dictionary
7. progress

DOWN

8. course
9. answer
10. reading
11. to learn

12. to study
13. lesson
14. homework
15. to understand

CHEZ LE COIFFEUR
AT THE HAIRDRESSER

28

AUDIO 28.1

Il – Elle a les cheveux ... | *He – she has ... hair*
Blancs adj | *White*
Blonds adj | *Blonde*
Bruns adj | *Brown*
Gris adj | *Grey*
Noirs adj | *Black*
Roux adj | *Red*

Il – elle est ... | *He – she is ...*
Blanc – Blanche adj | *White*
Blond – Blonde adj | *Blonde*
Brun – Brune adj | *Brown*
Gris – Grise adj | *Grey*
Noir – Noire adj | *Black*
Roux – Rousse adj | *Red-headed*

Les cheveux bouclés adj | *Curly hair*
Les cheveux courts adj | *Short hair*
Les cheveux longs adj | *Long hair*
Les cheveux ondulés adj | *Wavy hair*
Les cheveux raides – lisses adj | *Straight hair*

Un après-shampoing nm | *A conditioner*
Un balayage nm | *A balayage*
Une brosse nf | *A brush*
Un brushing nm | *A brushing*
Une chaise nf | *A chair*
Un chignon nm | *A bun*
Des ciseaux nm | *Scissors*
Un coiffeur – Une coiffeuse n | *A hairdresser*
Une coloration nf | *A color*
Une couleur nf | *A color*
Une coupe de cheveux nf | *A haircut*
Une frange nf | *Bangs*
Un magazine nm | *A magazine*
Un masque nm | *A mask*
Des mèches nf | *Highlights*
Un peigne nm | *A comb*
Une permanente nf | *A perm*
Des pinces nf | *Clips*
Les pointes nf | *The ends*
Un rasoir électrique nm | *An electric razor*
Un rendez-vous nm | *An appointment*
Un sèche-cheveux nm | *A hairdryer*
Un shampoing nm | *A shampoo*
Un traitement nm | *A treatment*

Aller bien v | *To suit*
Couper v | *To cut*
Laver v | *To wash*

Ajoutez **le bon mot** ou **groupe de mots** à chaque phrase.
Add the correct word or group of words to each sentence.

bien – **brushing** – **ciseaux** – **coiffeuse** – **coloration** – **coupe de cheveux** – **courts** –
frange – **magazines** – **cheveux** – **pointes** – **rasoir électrique** – **roux**

1. La ⬚⬚⬚ a coupé mes
   beaucoup trop ⬚⬚⬚.

2. Une ⬚⬚⬚ abîme les cheveux.

3. Cette ⬚⬚⬚ ne te va pas très ⬚⬚⬚.

4. Je lis toujours plusieurs ⬚⬚⬚ quand je suis chez le coiffeur.

5. Les cheveux ⬚⬚⬚ sont assez rares.

6. Elle a demandé au coiffeur de ne couper que les ⬚⬚⬚.

7. Le coiffeur utilise des ⬚⬚⬚ pour couper les cheveux.

8. Le coiffeur va me couper les cheveux d'abord, puis me faire un
   ⬚⬚⬚.

9. Elle coupe les cheveux de son mari avec un ⬚⬚⬚.

10. J'ai demandé une ⬚⬚⬚ mais je le regrette déjà.

TRANSLATION

1. *The hairdresser cut my hair way too short.*
2. *Coloring damages the hair.*
3. *This haircut doesn't suit you very well.*
4. *I always read several magazines when I'm at the hairdresser.*
5. *Red hair is quite rare.*
6. *She asked the hairdresser to only cut the ends.*
7. *The hairdresser uses scissors to cut hair.*
8. *The hairdresser will cut my hair first, then give me a brushing.*
9. *She cuts her husband's hair with an electric razor.*
10. *I asked for bangs, but I already regret it.*

LE CHIEN ET LE CHAT

DOG AND CAT

29

AUDIO 29.1 🔊

Le dos nm | *The back*
Les griffes nf | *Claws*
Le museau nm | *Nose*
Les pattes nf | *Paws*
La queue nf | *Tail*
La truffe nf | *Dog's nose*

La fourrure nf | *Fur*
Un poil nm | *A hair*

Un collier nm | *A collar*
Un harnais nm | *A harness*
Une laisse nf | *A leash*
Une promenade nf | *A walk*

Un bol – Une gamelle n | *A bowl*
Des croquettes nf | *Dry food*
De la nourriture nf | *Food*
De la pâtée nf | *Wet food*

Un éleveur nm | *A breeder*
Une race nf | *A breed*

Une balle nf | *A ball*
Un jouet nm | *A toy*
Un panier nm | *A dog bed*
Un tapis nm | *A carpet*

Caresser v | *To pet*
Dresser v | *To train*

Affectueux – Affectueuse adj | *Affectionate*
Apprivoisé – Apprivoisée adj | *Tamed*
Obéissant – Obéissante adj | *Obedient*
Gâté – Gâtée adj | *Spoiled*
Propre adj | *Clean – Trained*
Peureux – Peureuse adj | *Fearful*

AUDIO 29.2 🔊

Le chien – *The dog*

Un chien nm | *A male dog*
Une chienne nf | *A female dog*
Un chiot nm | *A puppy*
Un chien d'assistance nm | *A service dog*
Un chien guide nm | *A guide dog*

Promener le chien v | *To walk the dog*
Aboyer v | *To bark*
Le chien aboie | *The dog barks*

AUDIO 29.3 🔊

Le chat – *The cat*

Un chat nm | *A male cat*
Un chaton nm | *A kitten*
Une chatte nf | *A female cat*
Une boule de poils nf | *A hairball*
Les moustaches nf | *Whiskers*
Un arbre à chat nm | *A cat tree*
Un griffoir nm | *A scratching pole*

La litière nf | *Litter*

Miauler v | *To meow*
Le chat miaule | *The cat meows*
Ronronner v | *To purr*
Le chat ronronne | *The cat is purring*

Chosissez entre les **4 mots donnés** pour chaque phrase.
Choose between the 4 words given for each sentence.

1. **propre – gâté – peureux – content**

   Mon chat est _____ depuis qu'il est petit. Il se cache toujours quand j'ai des invités.

2. **dos – dents – yeux – queue**

   Le vétérinaire examine le _____ du chien vu qu'il a du mal à marcher.

3. **miaule – joue – caresse – ronronne**

   Son chat _____ quand il mange.

4. **croquettes – poils – pattes – jouets**

   Le chat a commencé à perdre ses _____ .

5. **manger – changer – jouer – promener**

   On essaye de _____ nos chiens 2 fois par jour.

6. **chiens guides – chiots – chiens d'assistance – chats**

   Les _____ sont importants pour les personnes malvoyantes.

7. **museau – queue – moustache – truffe**

   Un chien remue la _____ quand il est content.

8. **pâtée – croquette – litière – race**

   Mon chien et mon chat mangent de la _____ car ils n'ont plus de dents.

9. **yeux – pattes – dents – harnais**

   C'est bien de nettoyer les _____ du chien après une promenade.

10. **dresser – caresser – promener – aboyer**

    Les enfants du quartier veulent toujours _____ mon chien.

11. **gâtés – peureux – propres – affectueux**

    Ses animaux sont _____ . Ils ne manquent de rien.

12. **chien – chiot – éleveur – chat**

    Un _____ demande beaucoup d'attention jusqu'à l'âge adulte.

13. **laisse – litière – balle – harnais**

Notre chien a tellement grandi qu'il a besoin d'un nouveau   .

14. **fourrure – race – litière – croquette**

Il faut changer la   régulièrement pour qu'elle ne sente pas.

15. **miaule – aboie – joue – dresse**

Mon chat   toujours pour me réveiller le matin.

TRANSLATION

1. *My cat has been fearful since he was little. He always hides when I have guests.*
2. *The vet examines the dog's back as he has difficulty walking.*
3. *His cat purrs when he eats.*
4. *The cat started to lose his hair.*
5. *We try to walk our dogs twice a day.*
6. *Guide dogs are important for visually impaired people.*
7. *A dog wags his tail when he is happy.*
8. *My dog and my cat eat wet food because they no longer have teeth.*
9. *It's good to clean the dog's paws after a walk.*
10. *The neighborhood kids always want to pet my dog.*
11. *His animals are spoiled. They lack nothing.*
12. *A puppy requires a lot of attention until adulthood.*
13. *Our dog has grown so much that he needs a new harness.*
14. *You have to change the litter regularly, so it doesn't smell.*
15. *My cat always meows to wake me up in the morning.*

LE TEMPS
THE WEATHER

30

AUDIO 30.1 ◀))

La météo nf | *The weather*
Le temps nm | *The weather*

Quel temps fait-il ? | *How is the weather?*
Il fait beau | *It's nice out*
Il fait chaud | *It's hot*
Il fait frais | *It's cool – chilly*
Il fait froid | *It's cold*
Il fait humide | *It's humid*
Il fait lourd | *It's muggy*
Il fait mauvais | *It's bad weather*
Il fait nuageux | *It's cloudy*
Il fait orageux | *It's stormy*
Il fait soleil | *It's sunny*

Il fait 3 degrés | *It's 3 degrees*
Il fait moins 4 | *It's minus 4*

Il y a du brouillard | *It's foggy*
Il y a du soleil | *It's sunny*
Il y a du vent | *It's windy*
Il y a une tempête de neige | *It's a snowstorm*

Il gèle (geler) | *It's freezing (to freeze)*
Il grêle (grêler) | *It's hailing (to hail)*
Il neige (neiger) | *It's snowing (to snow)*
Il pleut (pleuvoir) | *It's raining (to rain)*

AUDIO 30.2 ◀))

Complétez les phrases avec **le vocabulaire** ci-dessus.
Complete the sentences with the vocabulary above.

1. Il y a une tempête, il y a du _____ .

2. Je ne vois pas la route devant moi, il y a du _____ .

3. Il fait chaud et il n'y a pas d'air, il fait _____ .

4. Les températures sont en-dessous de zéro, il _____ .

5. Tout est blanc dehors, il _____ .

Exercice personnel. Répondez aux questions et décrivez le temps.
Personal exercise. Answer the questions and describe the weather.

6. Aujourd'hui, il fait _____ .

7. Ce matin, il faisait _____ degrés.

8. Ce soir, il va faire ▨▨▨▨▨▨▨ degrés.

9. J'adore quand il fait ▨▨▨▨▨▨▨ .

10. Je déteste quand il fait ▨▨▨▨▨▨▨ .

TRANSLATION

1. *There's a storm, there's wind.*
2. *I can't see the road in front of me, it's foggy.*
3. *It's hot and there's no air, it's muggy.*
4. *The temperatures are below zero, it is freezing.*
5. *Everything is white outside, it's snowing.*
6. *Today, it is ▨▨▨▨▨▨▨ .*
7. *This morning, it was ▨▨▨▨▨▨▨ degrees.*
8. *Tonight, it will be ▨▨▨▨▨▨▨ degrees.*
9. *I love it when it's ▨▨▨▨▨▨▨ .*
10. *I hate it when it's ▨▨▨▨▨▨▨ .*

LE VISAGE
THE FACE

La bouche nf | *Mouth*
L'œil – Les yeux nm | *Eye(s)*
Une dent nf | *A tooth*
Le front nm | *Forehead*
Une joue nf | *A cheek*
Les lèvres nf | *Lips*
La mâchoire nf | *Jaw*
Le menton nm | *Chin*
Une narine nf | *A nostril*
Le nez nm | *Nose*
Les oreilles nf | *Ears*

La barbe nf | *Beard*
Les cheveux nm | *Hair*
La moustache nf | *Moustache*
Les sourcils nm | *Eyebrows*
Les cils nm | *Eyelashes*

 Ajoutez **le bon mot** à chaque phrase.
Add the right word to each sentence.

1. Il est chaud quand on est malade : le

2. Ils ont la même couleur que nos cheveux : les

3. On respire par la bouche ou par le

4. On peut y mettre du mascara : les

5. On voit avec les

6. On entend avec les

7. Elle pousse sur la partie basse du visage : la

8. On montre ses   quand on sourit.

9. La   bouge quand on parle.

10. Le nez a deux

TRANSLATION

1. *It's hot when you're sick: the forehead*
2. *They are the same color as our hair: eyebrows*
3. *We breathe through the mouth or nose.*
4. *You can put mascara on them: eyelashes*
5. *We see with our eyes.*
6. *We hear with our ears.*
7. *It grows on the lower part of the face: the beard*
8. *We show our teeth when we smile.*
9. *The jaw moves when we speak.*
10. *The nose has two nostrils.*

DANS MON FRIGO

IN MY FRIDGE

32

AUDIO 32.1 🔊

Les légumes – *Vegetables*

Du brocoli nm | *Broccoli*
Des carottes nf | *Carrots*
Du céleri nm | *Celery*
Des champignons nm | *Mushrooms*
Du chou-fleur nm | *Cauliflower*
Du concombre nm | *Cucumber*

De la courgette nm | *Zucchini*
Des épinards nm | *Spinach*
Des haricots verts nm | *Green beans*
Du maïs nm | *Corn*
Des petits pois nm | *Garden peas*
Du poireau nm | *Leek*

AUDIO 32.2 🔊

Les fruits – *Fruits*

Un avocat nm | *An avocado*
Des cerises nf | *Cherries*
Un citron nm | *A lemon*
Des fraises nf | *Strawberries*
Un kiwi nm | *A kiwi*
Un melon nm | *A melon*

Des olives nf | *Olives*
Une orange nf | *An orange*
Une pastèque nf | *A watermelon*
Une pêche nf | *A peach*
Une poire nf | *A pear*
Une pomme nf | *An apple*

AUDIO 32.3 🔊

Les produits laitiers – *Dairy Products*

Du beurre nm | *Butter*
De la crème nf | *Cream*
Du fromage nm | *Cheese*
Du fromage blanc nm | *Cream cheese*

Du fromage râpé nm | *Grated cheese*
Du lait nm | *Milk*
Du lait d'amande nm | *Almond milk*
Des yaourts nm | *Yogurts*

AUDIO 32.4 🔊

Les boissons – *Drinks*

De l'eau nf | *Water*
De l'eau pétillante nf | *Sparkling water*
De la bière nf | *Beer*

Du jus d'orange nm | *Orange juice*
Du vin blanc nm | *White wine*
Du vin rouge nm | *Red wine*

Les sauces – *Sauces*

Du ketchup nm | *Ketchup*
De la mayonnaise nf | *Mayonnaise*
De la moutarde nf | *Mustard*

De la vinaigrette nf | *Salad dressing*
De la sauce soja nf | *Soy sauce*
De la sauce piquante nf | *Hot sauce*

La viande, le poisson et les œufs – *Meat, Fish, and Eggs*

De la charcuterie nf | *Deli meat*
Des œufs nm | *Eggs*
Du poisson nm | *Fish*
De la viande nf | *Meat*

 Listez **20 choses** qui se trouvent dans votre frigo.
List 20 things that are in your fridge.

Dans mon frigo, il y a
In my fridge, there is

QUEL EST CE MOT ?
WHAT IS THIS WORD?

AUDIO 33.1 🔊

Remettez **les lettres** dans l'ordre pour trouver le bon mot. Aidez-vous **de l'indice** donné pour chaque mot.
Put the letters back in order to find the right word. Use the clue given for each word to help you.

1. **A B C E E L R T**

   On le place autour du poignet.
   It goes around the wrist.

2. **A A C E N R S S U**

   On la contacte après un accident.
   We contact them after an accident.

3. **E I O R S T T U**

   Une personne en vacances.
   A person on vacation.

4. **B E E I L L O T U**

   Un récipient pour liquide.
   A recipient for liquid.

5. **C C E E E M M M N N O T**

   C'est le début de tout.
   It's the start of everything.

6. **E E M M N O T U V**

   Il faut toujours bouger.
   We should always move.

7. **C E E E R T T**

   Pas à pas pour cuisiner.
   Step-by-step to cook.

8. **A B E O R T T U**

   Ce n'est pas une chaise.
   Not a chair.

9. **C É I I M N O O P T T**

   Que le meilleur gagne !
   May the best win!

10. **A A B C E I L O R U V**

    Plus on en a, mieux on parle.
    The more we have, the better we speak.

11. **A D E É N N N O R**

    Une longue marche.
    A long walk.

12. **A E O P P R S S T**

    On en a besoin pour voyager.
    We need it to travel.

---

13. A C D I N O R T T U

La même signification dans une autre langue.
The same meaning in another language.

14. A E É G N R R T

Une personne inconnue.
An unknown person.

15. A É I L L N P T T

Plein de bulles.
Full of bubbles.

L'ORDINATEUR

THE COMPUTER

AUDIO 34.1 🔊

Une adresse email nf | *An email address*
Une boîte de réception nf | *An inbox*
Un clavier nm | *A keyboard*
Un compte nm | *An account*
Un disque dur nm | *A hard drive*
Un dossier nm | *A folder*
Un écran nm | *A screen*
Une fenêtre nf | *A window*
Un fichier nm | *A file*
Un haut-parleur nm | *A speaker*
Une imprimante nf | *A printer*
L'informatique nm | *IT*
Internet nm | *The Internet*
Un logiciel nm | *A software*
La mémoire nf | *The memory*
Un mot de passe nm | *A password*
Un navigateur nm | *A browser*
Un ordinateur nm | *A computer*
Un ordinateur de bureau nm | *A desktop*
Un ordinateur portable nm | *A laptop*
Une page nf | *A page*
Un site internet nm | *A website*
Une souris nf | *A mouse*
Un tapis de souris nm | *A mouse pad*
Un utilisateur – Une utilisatrice n | *A user*

Allumer v | *To turn on*
Brancher v | *To plug*
Charger v | *To charge*
Cliquer v | *To click*
Coller v | *To paste*
Copier v | *To copy*
Éteindre v | *To turn off*
Imprimer v | *To print*
Installer v | *To install*
Rafraîchir v | *To refresh*

Redémarrer v | *To restart*
Sauvegarder v | *To save*
Taper v | *To type*
Télécharger v | *To download*

 Complétez le texte avec **les mots donnés** ci-dessous.
Complete the text with the words given below.

allumer – boîte de réception – charger – clavier – clique – comptes – écran – emails – éteins – imprimante – imprimer – mot de passe – ordinateur – pages – site internet – souris

Quand j'arrive au travail, je commence par _____ mon _____ . Je tape mon _____ . Quand mon ordinateur est allumé, j'ouvre ma _____ pour lire mes _____ . J'ai deux _____ différents, un pour mes emails privés et un pour mes emails professionnels. Après ça, je vérifie que mon _____ fonctionne. Je _____ sur quelques _____ pour vérifier les fonctionnalités. Après quelques heures, j'utilise l' _____ pour _____ des contrats. Mes yeux fatiguent vite à force de fixer l' _____ donc je fais une pause toutes les heures. À la fin de la journée, j' _____ mon ordinateur et je branche ma _____ et mon _____ pour les _____ .

TRANSLATION

When I arrive at work, I start by turning on my computer. I type my password. When my computer is on, I open my inbox to read my emails. I have two different accounts, one for my private emails and one for my professional emails. After that, I check that my website is working. I click through a few pages to check the features. After a few hours, I use the printer to print contracts. My eyes get tired quickly from staring at the screen so I take a break every hour. At the end of the day, I turn off my computer and plug in my mouse and my keyboard to charge.

Homophones are word that are pronounced the same but have different meanings. They can even have the same spelling sometimes. In this lesson, we are looking at 25 common French homophones.

AUDIO 35.1 🔊

Mal adj | *Wrong*
Le mal nm | *Evil – Pain*
Un mâle nm | *A male*
Une malle nf | *A trunk*

Mon adj | *My*
Le mont nm | *Mountain*

Un mur nm | *A wall*
Mûr adj | *Ripe*
Une mûre nf | *A blackberry*

Ni conj | *Neither*
Un nid nm | *A nest*

Le houx nm | *Holly*
Ou conj | *Or*
Où pr | *Where*

Une paie nf | *A pay*
La paix nf | *Peace*
Un pet nm | *A fart*

Un pain nm | *A loaf of bread*
Un pin nm | *A pine tree*

Pair adj | *Even*
Un pair nm | *A peer*
Une paire nf | *A pair*
Le père nm | *Father*

Par prep | *By*
Une part nf | *A part*

Un parti nm | *A political party*
Une partie nf | *A game*
Une partie nf | *A part*

La pâte nf | *Dough*
Les pâtes nf | *Pasta*
Une patte nf | *A paw*

Un poêle nm | *A stove*
Une poêle nf | *A pan*
Un poil nm | *A hair*

Le poids nm | *Weight*
Un pois nm | *A pea*

Le poing nm | *Fist*
Un point nm | *A point*

Le porc nm | *Pork*
Le port nm | *Harbor*

Près adv | *Near*
Prêt adj | *Ready*

Quand adv | *When*
Quant prep | *As for*
Un camp nm | *A camp*

Un saut nm | *A jump*
Un sceau nm | *A stamp*
Un seau nm | *A bucket*

Un sou nm | *A penny*
Sous prep | *Under*
Saoul adj | *Drunk*

Une tante nf | *An aunt*
Une tente nf | *A tent*

Le thon nm | *Tuna*
Ton adj | *Your*
Un ton nm | *A tone*

Un tic nm | *A tic*
Une tique nf | *A tick*

Vain adj | *Superficial*
Le vin nm | *Wine*
Vingt n | *Twenty*

Un ver nm | *A worm*
Un verre nm | *A glass*
Vers prep | *Toward*
Un vers nm | *A verse*
Vert adj | *Green*

Vu prep | *Given*
La vue nf | *Sight*

AUDIO 35.2 🔊

 Choisissez entre **les deux homophones** pour chaque phrase.
Choose between the two homophones for each sentence.

1. **Mon – Mont** –   rendez-vous vient d'être annulé.

2. **ni – nid** – Les oiseaux construisent un   dans l'arbre.

3. **pain – pin** – J'ai oublié d'acheter du   ce matin.

4. **par – part** – Tu devrais passer   ce village pour aller plus vite.

5. **pâte – patte** – Le chien s'est fait mal à la   en jouant.

6. **poêle – poil** – La   sur le four n'est pas propre.

7. **poids – pois** – Ce n'est pas grave si tu prends un peu de   .

8. **poing – point** – Il faut toujours ajouter un   à la fin d'une phrase.

9. **près – prêts** – On sera   dans une heure.

10. **saut – seau** – Je ne trouve pas le   pour nettoyer.

11. **sous – sou** – Il n'a pas un   dans son portefeuille.

12. **tante – tente** – Ma _____ vient passer le week-end chez nous.

13. **Vers – Vert** – _____ quelle heure est-ce que tu seras là ?

14. **vin – vingt** – Ce _____ est trop sucré pour moi.

15. **vu – vue** – Ma _____ n'a pas changé depuis mon dernier examen.

TRANSLATION

1. *My appointment has just been canceled.*
2. *The birds build a nest in the tree.*
3. *I forgot to buy bread this morning.*
4. *You should go through this village to go faster.*
5. *The dog hurt his paw while playing.*
6. *The pan on the oven is not clean.*
7. *It's okay if you gain a little weight.*
8. *You should always add a period at the end of a sentence.*
9. *We'll be ready in an hour.*
10. *I can't find the bucket to clean.*
11. *He doesn't have a penny in his wallet.*
12. *My aunt is coming to spend the weekend with us.*
13. *Around what time will you be there?*
14. *This wine is too sweet for me.*
15. *My vision has not changed since my last exam.*

LES ANIMAUX

ANIMALS

36

AUDIO 36.1 ◄))

Un agneau nm | *A lamb*
Un âne nm | *A donkey*
Un canard nm | *A duck*
Un castor nm | *A beaver*
Un cerf nm | *A deer*
Un chat nm | *A cat*
Une chauve-souris nf | *A bat*
Un cheval nm | *A horse*
Une chèvre nf | *A goat*
Un chien nm | *A dog*
Une chouette nf | *An owl*
Un cochon d'inde nm | *A guinea pig*
Un cochon nm | *A pig*
Un coq nm | *A rooster*
Un coyote nm | *A coyote*
Une dinde nf | *A turkey*
Un écureuil nm | *A squirrel*
Un élan nm | *A moose*
Un hamster nm | *A hamster*
Un hérisson nm | *A hedgehog*
Un lapin nm | *A rabbit*

Un lézard nm | *A lizard*
Un loup nm | *A wolf*
Un lynx nm | *A lynx*
Une moufette nf | *A skunk*
Un mouton nm | *A sheep*
Un ours nm | *A bear*
Un perroquet nm | *A parrot*
Un poisson rouge nm | *A goldfish*
Un poney nm | *A pony*
Une poule nf | *A hen*
Un poussin nm | *A chick*
Un raton laveur nm | *A raccoon*
Un renard nm | *A fox*
Un sanglier nm | *A wild boar*
Une souris nf | *A mouse*
Un taureau nm | *A bull*
Une tortue nf | *A turtle*
Une vache nf | *A cow*
Un veau nm | *A calf*
Une volaille nf | *Poultry*

AUDIO 36.2 ◄))

 Quel est **l'animal décrit** dans chaque phrase ?
What animal is described in each sentence?

1. C'est le petit de la poule : un

2. C'est un animal domestique qui aboie : un

3. C'est un animal qui miaule et aime les caresses : un

4. C'est un petit animal à carapace qui marche lentement : une

5. C'est un oiseau qui imite les voix humaines : un

6. C'est un animal nocturne qui a de grands yeux : une

7. C'est un petit animal qui vit dans les arbres et adore les noisettes :
    un

8. C'est un animal sauvage qui ressemble à un gros chien et vit en meute :
    un

9. C'est un mammifère aquatique qui construit des barrages : un

10. C'est un animal qui se met en boule pour se protéger : un

11. C'est un animal herbivore qui a des bois sur sa tête : un

12. C'est un animal qui peut nager et aime les mares : un

13. C'est un petit rongeur qui adore les carottes : un

14. C'est un reptile qui change de peau et aime le soleil : un

15. C'est un animal qui n'aime pas la couleur rouge : un

TRANSLATION

1. *It's the hen's baby: a chick*
2. *It's a domestic animal that barks: a dog*
3. *It's an animal that meows and likes pets: a cat*
4. *It's a small shelled animal that walks slowly: a turtle*
5. *It's a bird that imitates human voices: a parrot*
6. *It is a nocturnal animal that has big eyes: an owl*
7. *It's a small animal that lives in trees and loves nuts: a squirrel*
8. *It is a wild animal that resembles a large dog and lives in packs: a wolf*
9. *It's an aquatic mammal that builds dams: a beaver*
10. *It's an animal that curls up into a ball to protect itself: a hedgehog*
11. *It is a herbivorous animal that has antlers on its head: a deer*
12. *It is a animal that can swim and likes ponds: a duck*
13. *It's a small rodent that loves carrots: a rabbit*
14. *It's a reptile that changes skin and loves the sun: a lizard*
15. *It's an animal that doesn't like the color red: a bull*

LES PASSE-TEMPS
HOBBIES

AUDIO 37.1 🔊

Aller au cinéma | *To go to the theater*
Collectionner les pièces de monnaie | *To collect coins*
Coudre ses vêtements | *To sew clothes*
Écouter de la musique | *To listen to music*
Étudier les langues | *To study languages*
Faire de la calligraphie | *To practice calligraphy*
Faire de la danse – Danser | *To dance*
Faire de la menuiserie | *To do woodworking*
Faire de la pâtisserie | *To bake*
Faire de la peinture – Peindre | *To paint*
Faire de la philatélie | *To collect stamps*
Faire de la photographie | *To do photography*
Faire de la poterie | *To do pottery*
Faire de la randonnée | *To hike*
Faire de la sculpture | *To sculpt*
Faire des bijoux | *To make jewelry*
Faire du camping – Camper | *To camp*
Faire du chant – Chanter | *To sing*
Faire du crochet | *To crochet*
Faire du cyclisme | *To bike*
Faire du dessin – Dessiner | *To draw*
Faire du jardinage – Jardiner | *To garden*
Faire du savon | *To make soap*
Faire du shopping | *To go shopping*
Faire du sport – de l'exercice | *To exercise*
Faire du théâtre | *To play*
Faire du tricot – Tricoter | *To knit*
Faire la cuisine – Cuisiner | *To cook*
Faire des mots croisés | *To do crosswords*
Faire un puzzle | *To make a puzzle*
Jouer aux échecs | *To play chess*
Jouer aux jeux de société | *To play board games*
Jouer aux jeux vidéo | *To play video games*
Jouer de la musique | *To play music*
Lire | *To read*
Regarder la télévision | *To watch TV*

Le cinéma nm | *Theater*
Une collection nf | *A collection*
La couture nf | *Sewing*
La musique nf | *Music*
Les langues nf | *Languages*
La calligraphie nf | *Calligraphy*
La danse nf | *Dancing*
La menuiserie nf | *Woodworking*
La pâtisserie nf | *Baking*
La peinture nf | *Painting*
La philatélie nf | *Stamp collecting*
La photographie nf | *Photography*
La poterie nf | *Pottery*
La randonnée nf | *Hiking*
La sculpture nf | *Sculpting*
Les bijoux nm | *Jewelry making*
Le camping nm | *Camping*
Le chant nm | *Singing*
Le crochet nm | *Crocheting*
Le vélo nm | *Bike riding*
Le dessin nm | *Drawing*
Le jardinage nm | *Gardening*
Le savon nm | *Soap making*
Le shopping nm | *Shopping*
Le sport – L'exercice nm | *Exercising*
L'art dramatique nm | *Acting*
Le tricot nm | *Knitting*
La cuisine nf | *Cooking*
Les mots croisés nm | *Crosswords*
Un puzzle nm | *A puzzle*
Les échecs nm | *Chess*
Les jeux de société nm | *Boardgames*
Les jeux vidéo nm | *Video games*
La musique nf | *Music*
La lecture nf | *Reading*
La télévision nf | *TV*

Quel est **le verbe** qui correspond à chaque passe-temps ?
What verb corresponds to each pastime?

1. La couture

2. Les langues

3. La danse

4. La peinture

5. Le camping

6. Le chant

7. Le dessin

8. Le jardinage

9. Le tricot

10. La cuisine

11. La lecture

AUDIO 37.3 ◀ᴿ)

 Quels sont **vos passe-temps** ?
What are your hobbies?

Pendant mon temps libre, j'aime

LA FRÉQUENCE
FREQUENCY

38

AUDIO 38.1 🔊

Plusieurs fois par jour	*Several times a day*
Une fois par jour	*Once a day*
Plusieurs fois par semaine	*Several times a week*
Une fois par semaine	*Once a week*
Plusieurs fois par mois	*Several times a month*
Une fois par mois	*Once a month*
Plusieurs foir par an	*Several times a year*
Une fois par an	*Once a year*
Jamais	*Never*

AUDIO 38.2 🔊

À quelle **fréquence** est-ce que vous faites **les activités** ci-dessous ?
How often do you do the activities below?

1. J'assiste à un concert.

2. J'écoute de la musique.

3. J'écris à / Je parle avec mes amis et ma famille.

4. J'organise un barbecue.

5. Je bois du café.

6. Je fais du camping.

7. Je fais du shopping.

8. Je fais du sport.

9. Je fais la lessive.

10. Je fais les courses.

11. Je fais mon lit.

12. Je fais un road trip.

13. Je fais une randonnée.

14. Je jardine.

15. Je lis / Je regarde les nouvelles.

16. Je lis un livre.

17. Je me brosse les dents.

18. Je nettoie la maison.

19. Je participe à un cours de cuisine.

20. Je prends le bus.

21. Je prends une douche.

22. Je prépare le petit déjeuner.

23. Je regarde la télévision.

24. Je rends visite à ma famille.

25. Je sors les poubelles.

26. Je vais à la plage.

27. Je vais au restaurant.

28. Je vais au travail.

29. Je vais en vacances.

30. Je visite un musée.

AUDIO 38.3 ◄))

VOCABULARY

Assister v | *To attend*
Un concert nm | *A concert*
Écouter v | *To listen*
De la musique nf | *Music*
Écrire v | *To write*
Parler v | *To speak*
Un ami – Une amie n | *A friend*
Une famille nf | *A family*

Organiser v | *To organize*
Un barbecue nm | *A barbecue*
Boire v | *To drink*
Un café nm | *A coffee*
Faire v | *To do*
Du camping nm | *Camping*
Du shopping nm | *Shopping*
Du sport nm | *Sport*

La **lessive** nf | *The laundry*
Les **courses** nf | *Grocery shopping*
Un **lit** nm | *A bed*
Un **road trip** nm | *A road trip*
Une **randonnée** nf | *A hike*
Jardiner v | *To garden*
Lire v | *To read*
Regarder v | *To watch*
Les **nouvelles** nf | *The news*
Un **livre** nm | *A book*
Se **brosser** v | *To brush*
Les **dents** nf | *The teeth*
Nettoyer v | *To clean*
La **maison** nf | *The house*
Participer v | *To participate*
Un **cours de cuisine** nm | *A cooking class*
Prendre v | *To take*

Le **bus** nm | *The bus*
Une **douche** nf | *A shower*
Préparer v | *To prepare*
Le **petit déjeuner** nm | *Breakfast*
Regarder v | *To watch*
La **télévision** nf | *Television*
Rendre visite v | *To visit*
Sortir v | *To take out*
Les **poubelles** nf | *The trash*
Aller v | *To go*
La **plage** nf | *The beach*
Un **restaurant** nm | *A restaurant*
Le **travail** nm | *Work*
Les **vacances** nf | *Vacations*
Visiter v | *To visit*
Un **musée** nm | *A museum*

TRANSLATION

1. *I attend a concert.*
2. *I listen to music.*
3. *I write to/talk to my friends and family.*
4. *I have a barbecue.*
5. *I drink coffee.*
6. *I camp.*
7. *I go shopping.*
8. *I workout.*
9. *I do the laundry.*
10. *I shop.*
11. *I make my bed.*
12. *I go on a road trip.*
13. *I take a hike.*
14. *I garden.*
15. *I read/watch the news.*

16. *I read a book.*
17. *I brush my teeth.*
18. *I clean the house.*
19. *I take a cooking class.*
20. *I take the bus.*
21. *I take a shower.*
22. *I prepare the breakfast.*
23. *I watch TV.*
24. *I visit my family.*
25. *I take out the trash.*
26. *I go to the beach.*
27. *I go to the restaurant.*
28. *I go to work.*
29. *I go on vacation.*
30. *I visit a museum.*

Below you can find 40 words related to the house. Read and study the vocabulary before filling up the crossword or challenge yourself and try directly the crossword.

AUDIO 39.1 ◄))

Une armoire nf | *A wardrobe*
Une baignoire nf | *A bathtub*
Un canapé nm | *A couch*
La cave nf | *The cellar*
Une chaise nf | *A chair*
La chambre nf | *The bedroom*
Un congélateur nm | *A freezer*
Le couloir nm | *The corridor*
La cuisine nf | *The kitchen*
Une cuisinière nf | *A stove*
Une douche nf | *A shower*
Les escaliers nm | *The stairs*
Une étagère nf | *A shelf*
Un évier nm | *A sink*
Un fauteuil nm | *An armchair*
Un four nm | *An oven*
Le garage nm | *The garage*
Le grenier nm | *The attic*
Le jardin nm | *The garden*
Une lampe nf | *The lamp*
Un lave-linge nm | *A washing machine*
Un lave-vaisselle nm | *A dishwasher*
Un lit nm | *A bed*
La maison nf | *The house*
Un micro-ondes nm | *A microwave*
Un ordinateur nm | *A computer*

Un placard nm | *A closet*
Un réfrigérateur nm | *A refrigerator*
Des rideaux nm | *Curtains*
Un robinet nm | *A tap*
La salle à manger nf | *The dining room*
La salle de bain nf | *The bathroom*
Le salon nm | *The living room*
Un sèche-linge nm | *A dryer*
Une table nf | *A table*
Un tableau nm | *A painting*
Un tapis nm | *A carpet*
Une télévision nf | *A television*
Les toilettes nf | *The toilets*
Un ventilateur nm | *A fan*

Ajoutez la traduction de chaque mot dans **les cases numérotées**. Pour les noms, ajoutez seulement le nom et pas l'article.

Add the translation of each word in the numbered boxes. For nouns, add only the noun and not the article.

ACROSS

1. table

2. couch

3. computer

4. garage

5. bedroom

6. corridor

DOWN

7. bed

8. wardrobe

9. shower

10. cellar

11. chair

12. living room

13. armchair

14. tap

15. carpet

VRAI OU FAUX
TRUE OR FALSE

40

AUDIO 40.1 🔊

Voici **20 faits** de connaissance générale. Écrivez **Vrai (V)** ou **Faux (F)** devant chaque phrase. Le vocabulaire est listé après l'exercice.
Here are 20 facts about common knowledge. Write Vrai (V) or Faux (F) in front of each sentence. The vocabulary is listed after the exercise.

1.   Le Louvre est un musée situé à Paris.

2.   Les kangourous vivent en Amérique du Nord.

3.   L'Amazonie est la plus grande forêt tropicale du monde.

4.   La Joconde a été peinte par Van Gogh.

5.   Les koalas mangent principalement des feuilles d'eucalyptus.

6.   Le Mexique se trouve en Europe.

7.   La Tour de Pise est célèbre pour son inclinaison.

8.   Le plus petit pays du monde est le Vatican.

9.   Les zèbres ont des rayures noires et blanches.

10.   Le français est la langue officielle de l'Allemagne.

11.   La Statue de la Liberté a été offerte par la France.

12.   La population mondiale dépasse les 10 milliards.

13.   Les arbres produisent de l'oxygène.

14.   Le chocolat est fabriqué à partir de fèves de cacao.

15.   Le premier homme à marcher sur la lune était Neil Armstrong.

16.   Le cinéma a été inventé par les frères Lumière.

17.   Les échecs sont un jeu de société.

18.   Les diamants peuvent être fabriqués en laboratoire.

19. _____ La Saint-Valentin est en septembre.

20. _____ Pour obtenir la couleur rose, on mélange du rouge et du jaune.

VOCABULARY

Un musée nm | *A museum*
Se situer v | *To be located*
Un kangourou nm | *A kangaroo*
Vivre v | *To live*
L'Amérique du Nord nf | *North America*
L'Amazonie nf | *The Amazon*
Une forêt tropicale nf | *A tropical rainforest*
Le monde nm | *The world*
La Joconde nf | *The Mona Lisa*
Un koala nm | *A koala*
Manger v | *To eat*
Une feuille d'eucalyptus nf | *A eucalyptus leaf*
Le Mexique nm | *Mexico*
Se trouver v | *To be located*
L'Europe nf | *Europe*
La Tour de Pise nf | *The Leaning Tower*
Célèbre adj | *Famous*
Une inclinaison nf | *A tilt*
Le plus petit | *The smallest*
Un pays nm | *A country*
Un zèbre nm | *A zebra*
Une rayure nf | *A stripe*
Noir – Noire adj | *Black*
Blanc – Blanche adj | *White*
Le français nm | *French*
La langue officielle nf | *The official language*
L'Allemagne nf | *Germany*
La Statue de la Liberté nf | *The Statue of Liberty*
La France nf | *France*
La population mondiale nf | *The world population*
Dépasser v | *To exceed*
Un milliard nm | *A billion*
Un arbre nm | *A tree*
Produire v | *To produce*
De l'oxygène nf | *Oxygen*

Le chocolat nm | *Chocolate*
Être fabriqué(e) v | *To be made*
Une fève de cacao nf | *A cocoa bean*
Le premier homme | *The first man*
Marcher v | *To walk*
La Lune nf | *The moon*
Le cinéma nm | *Cinema*
Un frère nm | *A brother*
Les échecs nm | *Chess*
Un jeu de société nm | *A board game*

Un diamant nm | *A diamond*
Un laboratoire nm | *A laboratory*
La Saint-Valentin nf | *Valentine's Day*
Septembre nm | *September*
Obtenir v | *To get*
Une couleur nf | *A color*
Le rose nm | *Pink*
Mélanger v | *To mix*
Le rouge nm | *Red*
Le jaune nm | *Yellow*

TRANSLATION

1. *The Louvre is a museum located in Paris.*

2. *Kangaroos live in North America.*

3. *The Amazon is the largest tropical rainforest in the world.*

4. *The Mona Lisa was painted by Van Gogh.*

5. *Koalas primarily eat eucalyptus leaves.*

6. *Mexico is located in Europe.*

7. *The Leaning Tower of Pisa is famous for its tilt.*

8. *The smallest country in the world is the Vatican.*

9. *Zebras have black and white stripes.*

10. *French is the official language of Germany.*

11. *The Statue of Liberty was gifted by France.*

12. *The world population exceeds 10 billion.*

13. *Trees produce oxygen.*

14. *Chocolate is made from cocoa beans.*

15. *The first man to walk on the moon was Neil Armstrong.*

16. *Cinema was invented by the Lumière brothers.*

17. *Chess is a board game.*

18. *Diamonds can be made in a laboratory.*

19. *Valentine's Day is in September.*

20. *To get the color pink, mix red and yellow.*

LES VERBES ET LEURS CONTRAIRES
VERBS AND THEIR OPPOSITES

41

AUDIO 41.1 ◄))

When a verb starts with *a consonant*, its opposite will take *dé-* at the beginning.

Boutonner v | *To button*	**Déboutonner** v | *To unbutton*
Brancher v | *To plug*	**Débrancher** v | *To unplug*
Charger v | *To load*	**Décharger** v | *To unload*
Coincer v | *To stick*	**Décoincer** v | *To unstick*
Connecter v | *To connect*	**Déconnecter** v | *To disconnect*
Conseiller v | *To advise*	**Déconseiller** v | *To advise against*
Couvrir v | *To cover*	**Découvrir** v | *To uncover*
Faire v | *To do*	**Défaire** v | *To undo*
Froisser v | *To crumple*	**Défroisser** v | *To smooth out*
Gonfler v | *To inflate*	**Dégonfler** v | *To deflate*
Se maquiller v | *To put on makeup*	**Se démaquiller** v | *To remove makeup*
Monter v | *To assemble*	**Démonter** v | *To disassemble*
Plier v | *To fold*	**Déplier** v | *To unfold*
Ranger v | *To tidy*	**Déranger** v | *To mess up*
Verrouiller v | *To lock*	**Déverrouiller** v | *To unlock*

AUDIO 41.2 ◄))

When a verb starts with *a vowel*, its opposite will take *dés-* at the beginning.

S'abonner v | *To subscribe*	**Se désabonner** v | *To unsubscribe*
Activer v | *To activate*	**Désactiver** v | *To deactivate*
Approuver v | *To approve*	**Désapprouver** v | *To disapprove*
Armer v | *To arm*	**Désarmer** v | *To disarm*
Embarquer v | *To embark*	**Désembarquer** v | *To disembark*
Équilibrer v | *To balance*	**Déséquilibrer** v | *To unbalance*
S'habiller v | *To dress*	**Se déshabiller** v | *To undress*
Humidifier v | *To humidify*	**Déshumidifier** v | *To dehumidify*
S'hydrater v | *To hydrate*	**Se déshydrater** v | *To dehydrate*
Infecter v | *To infect*	**Désinfecter** v | *To disinfect*
Installer v | *To install*	**Désinstaller** v | *To uninstall*
Obéir v | *To obey*	**Désobéir** v | *To disobey*

Trouvez **l'infinitif du verbe** dans la phrase et ajoutez **le contraire du verbe**.
Find the infinitive of the verb in the sentence and add the opposite of the verb.

1. J'ai coincé la tirette de mon manteau.

   Infinitif :   Contraire :

2. Il s'est abonné à plusieurs magazines.

   Infinitif :   Contraire :

3. Je plie les vêtements avant de les ranger.

   Infinitif :   Contraire :

4. Elles se maquillent tous les jours.

   Infinitif :   Contraire :

5. Les voyageurs sont en train d'embarquer.

   Infinitif :   Contraire :

6. N'oublie pas de boutonner ta chemise.

   Infinitif :   Contraire :

7. Il gonfle le ballon de plage pour ses enfants.

   Infinitif :   Contraire :

8. C'est important de s'hydrater quand il fait chaud.

   Infinitif :   Contraire :

9. L'informaticien installe le nouveau serveur.

   Infinitif :   Contraire :

10. Il me conseille d'économiser plus pour acheter une maison.

    Infinitif :   Contraire :

11. J'ai approuvé le budget du nouveau projet.

Infinitif :   Contraire :

12. On doit charger la voiture avant de partir.

Infinitif :   Contraire :

13. Est-ce que tu as verrouillé la porte ?

Infinitif :   Contraire :

14. Les enfants obéissent à leurs parents.

Infinitif :   Contraire :

15. Mon père monte la nouvelle bibliothèque dans le garage.

Infinitif :   Contraire :

TRANSLATION

1. *I got my coat zipper stuck.*
2. *He subscribes to several magazines.*
3. *I fold clothes before putting them away.*
4. *They wear makeup every day.*
5. *Passengers are boarding.*
6. *Don't forget to button your shirt.*
7. *He inflates the beach ball for his children.*
8. *It's important to hydrate when it's hot.*
9. *The IT specialist installs the new server.*
10. *He advises me to save more to buy a house.*
11. *I approved the budget for the new project.*
12. *We have to load the car before leaving.*
13. *Did you lock the door?*
14. *Children obey their parents.*
15. *My father is assembling the new bookcase in the garage.*

LES VOYAGES
TRAVELS

42

AUDIO 42.1 🔊

Aller v | *To go*
Louer v | *To rent*
Partir en vacances | *To go on vacation*
Partir v | *To leave*
Réserver v | *To book*
Voyager v | *To travel*

Un aéroport nm | *An airport*
Un – Une agent de voyage n | *A travel agent*
Un appareil photo nm | *A camera*
L'arrivée nf | *Arrival*
Un avion nm | *A plane*
Un bagage à main nm | *A carry-on*
Un bagage nm | *A baggage*
Le camping nm | *Camping*
Une caravane nf | *A caravan*
Une carte de crédit nf | *A credit card*
Une carte nf | *A map*
Une croisière nf | *A cruise*
Le départ nm | *Departure*
Une destination nf | *A destination*
La douane nf | *Customs*
Une excursion nf | *An excursion*
Un guide nm | *A guide*
Un hôtel nm | *A hotel*
Un itinéraire nm | *A route*
Le métro nm | *The subway*
Un motel nm | *A motel*
Un musée nm | *A museum*

Un passager – Une passagère n | *A passenger*
Un passeport nm | *A passport*
Une piscine nm | *A pool*
Un safari nm | *A safari*
Un souvenir nm | *A souvenir*
Un taxi nm | *A taxi*
Les vacances nf | *Holidays*
Un visa nm | *A visa*
Une visite nf | *A tour*

Faire sa valise v | *To pack*
Un chapeau nm | *A hat*
De la crème solaire nf | *Sunscreen*
Un livre nm | *A book*
Des lunettes de soleil nf | *Sunglasses*
Un maillot de bain nm | *A swimsuit*
Un sac de plage nm | *A beach bag*
Des sandales nf | *Sandals*
Une serviette de plage nf | *A beach towel*
Un short nm | *A pair of shorts*
Un t-shirt nm | *A t-shirt*
Des tongs nf | *Flip-flops*
Une valise nf | *A suitcase*

Complétez le texte avec **les mots donnés** ci-dessous.
Complete the text with the words given below.

a loué – a réservé – avion – chapeau – faire ma valise – guide – hôtel – livre – maillot de bain – part en vacances – piscine – va – visiter – visites – voyages

Mon mari et moi, on _____ demain matin. On

_____ en Italie. Notre _____

est à 9 heures du matin. On _____ une semaine dans un

_____ près de la plage et on _____

une voiture. Je dois encore _____ ce soir. J'ai déjà préparé

tous mes habits d'été. Le plus important est mon _____

car j'adore me baigner, un _____ pour lire au soleil, et

un _____ pour protéger ma tête du soleil. Quand on sera

à l'hôtel, on demandera s'ils connaissent un _____ pour

_____ la vieille ville. On essaye toujours de faire une ou deux

_____ durant nos _____. Le reste du

temps, on le passe à se reposer au bord de la _____.

TRANSLATION

My husband and I are going on vacation tomorrow morning. We're going to Italy. Our plane is at 9 a.m. We booked a week in a hotel near the beach and rented a car. I still have to pack my suitcase this evening. I have already prepared all my summer clothes. The most important thing is my swimsuit because I love swimming, a book to read in the sun, and a hat to protect my head from the sun. When we get to the hotel, we will ask if they know a guide to visit the old town. We always try to make one or two visits during our trips. The rest of the time is spent relaxing by the pool.

QUELLE EST LA BONNE ORTHOGRAPHE ?

43

WHAT IS THE RIGHT SPELLING?

AUDIO 43.1 ◀))

Let's test your spelling in French!

 Choisissez **la bonne orthographe** parmi les deux mots donnés
Choose the right spelling among the two spellings given.

1. **travail – travaille** – Je commence toujours le   à 9 heures.

2. **bonbon – bombon** – Est-ce que tu veux un   ?

3. **environnement – envirronnement** – C'est important de prendre soin de l'   .

4. **dîner – dînner** – Le   est servi.

5. **attrapper – attraper** – Tu vas   froid si tu ne te couvres pas.

6. **appellé – appelé** – On a   le voisin mais il n'a pas répondu.

7. **feuilles – fueilles** – J'ai besoin de plus de   de papier.

8. **addition – addission** – Est-ce que je peux avoir l'   ?

9. **siences – sciences** – J'aime les   mais je ne veux pas travailler dans ce domaine.

10. **toillettes – toilettes** – Les   sont hors service.

11. **ascenseur – ascenceur** – L'   peut accueillir 10 personnes en même temps.

12. **ambulance – anbulance** – L'   est arrivée en moins de trente minutes.

13. **envelloppe – enveloppe** – Il y a une   dans la boîte aux lettres.

14. **automne – autome** – L'   a déjà commencé.

15. **deuzième – deuxième** – C'est la   fois qu'on te le demande.

VOCABULARY

Commencer v | *To start*
Le travail nm | *Work*
Un bonbon nm | *A candy*
Important – Importante adj | *Important*
Prendre soin de v | *To take care of*
L'environnement nm | *The environment*
Le dîner nm | *Dinner*
Être servi(e) v | *To be served*
Attraper froid | *To catch a cold*
Se couvrir v | *To cover up*
Appeler v | *To call*
Un voisin nm | *Dinner*
Répondre v | *To answer*
Avoir besoin de v | *To need*
Une feuille de papier nf | *A piece of paper*
Une addition nf | *A bill*

Les sciences nf | *Sciences*
Travailler v | *To work*
Un domaine nm | *A field*
Les toilettes nf | *Toilets*
Hors service adj | *Out of order*
Un ascenseur nm | *An elevator*
Accueillir v | *To welcome*
Une personne nf | *A person*
Une ambulance nf | *An ambulance*
Une minute nf | *A minute*
Une enveloppe nf | *An envelope*
Une boîte aux lettres nf | *A mailbox*
L'automne nm | *Fall/Autumn*
Commencer v | *To start*
Deuxième | *Second*
Demander v | *To ask*

TRANSLATION

1.   *I always start work at 9 o'clock.*

2.   *Do you want a candy?*

3.   *It's important to take care of the environment.*

4.   *Dinner is served.*

5.   *You'll catch a cold if you don't cover up.*

6.   *We called the neighbor but he didn't answer.*

7.   *I need more sheets of paper.*

8.   *Can I have the bill?*

9.   *I like science but I don't want to work in this field.*

10.   *The toilets are out of service.*

11.   *The elevator can accommodate 10 people at the same time.*

12.   *The ambulance arrived in less than thirty minutes.*

13.   *There is an envelope in the mailbox.*

14.   *Fall has already begun.*

15.   *This is the second time you've been asked this.*

LE TEMPS

TIME

44

Une seconde nf | *A second*
Une minute nf | *A minute*
Un quart d'heure nm | *A quarter of an hour*
Une demi-heure nf | *Half an hour*
Une heure nf | *An hour*
Un jour nm | *A day*
Une journée nf | *A day*
Une semaine nf | *A week*
Un mois nm | *A month*
Un trimestre nm | *A trimester*
Un semestre nm | *A semester*
Un an nm | *A year*
Une année nf | *A year*
Une décennie nf | *A decade*
Un siècle nm | *A century*
Un millénaire nm | *A millennium*

Un matin nm | *A morning*
Un après-midi nm | *An afternoon*
Une soirée nf | *An evening*
Une nuit nf | *A night*

Midi nm | *Noon*
Minuit nm | *Midnight*

Le crépuscule nm | *Dusk*
L'aube nf | *Dawn*

L'année dernière | *Last year*
Le mois dernier | *Last month*
La semaine dernière | *Last week*
Avant-hier adv | *The day before yesterday*
La veille de | *The day before (in the past)*
Hier adv | *Yesterday*
Aujourd'hui adv | *Today*
Maintenant adv | *Now*
Demain adv | *Tomorrow*
Après-demain adv | *The day after tomorrow*
Le lendemain de | *The day after (in the future)*
La semaine prochaine | *Next week*
Le mois prochain | *Next month*
L'année prochaine | *Next year*

 Ajoutez **le bon mot** à chaque phrase.
Add the correct word to each sentence.

1. Il y a 60 _____ dans une minute.

2. Il y a 24 _____ dans une journée.

3. Il y a 7 _____ dans une semaine.

4. Un _____ compte 4 ou 5 semaines.

5. Il y a 10 _____ dans une décennie.

Aujourd'hui, nous sommes le 1er décembre. Ajoutez les références de temps à chaque phrase en fonction de la date d'aujourd'hui.
Today is December 1st. Add time references to each sentence based on today's date.

6. Il y a 7 jours, c'était la semaine   .

7.   , c'était le 29 novembre.

8.   , c'était le 30 novembre.

9.   , ça sera le 2 décembre.

10.   , ça sera le 3 décembre.

11. Dans 7 jours, ça sera la semaine   .

TRANSLATION

1. *There are 60 seconds in a minute.*
2. *There are 24 hours in a day.*
3. *There are 7 days in a week.*
4. *A month has 4 or 5 weeks.*
5. *There are 10 years in a decade.*

Today is December 1st.

6. *7 days ago was last week.*
7. *The day before yesterday was November 29th.*
8. *Yesterday was November 30th.*
9. *Tomorrow will be December 2nd.*
10. *The day after tomorrow will be December 3rd.*
11. *In 7 days, it will be next week.*

LES MOTS ANGLAIS UTILISÉS EN FRANÇAIS

45

ENGLISH WORDS USED IN FRENCH

AUDIO 45.1 🔊

Un **airbag** nm

ASAP (As soon as possible)

Un – Une **baby-sitter** n

Du **bacon** nm

Un **bar** nm

Un **barbecue** nm

Le **basketball** nm

Un **best-seller** nm

Le **bowling** nm

Un **building** nm

Le **business** nm

Un **casting** nm

Un **challenge** nm

Le **chat** nm

Un **clown** nm

Un **coach** nm

Un **cocktail** nm

Un **cowboy** nm

Un **crash** nm

Un **design** nm

Un **discount** nm

Le **drive-in** nm

Une **exit** nf

Un **ferry** nm

Le **fitness** nm

Un **flash-back** nm

Un **flyer** nm

Un **follower** nm

Le **football** nm

Fun adj

Un **hashtag** nm

Un **holdup** nm

Un **interview** nm

Un **jackpot** nm

Un **jean** nm

Un **job** nm

Un **kidnapping** nm

Un **kit** nm

Un **laptop** nm

Un **laser** nm

Les **news** nf

Un **living room** nm

Low-cost adj

Un **manager** nm

Le **marketing** nm

Un **match** nm

Un **meeting** nm

Non-stop adj

Open adj

Un **pacemaker** nm

Un **parking** nm

Un **pickpocket** nm

Le **planning** nm

Une **playlist** nf

Le **pop-corn** nm

Un **post** nm

Un **sandwich** nm

Le **self-service** nm

Un **selfie** nm

Un **serial killer** nm

Le **shopping** nm

Un **show** nm

Un **sketch** nm

Un **smartphone** nm

Un **spam** nm

Une **star** nf

Un sticker nm

Un supporter nm

Un teaser nm

Le tennis nm

Un thriller nm

Le timing nm

Vintage adj

Le week-end nm

Un workshop nm

AUDIO 45.2 ◄))

 Complétez les phrases avec **les mots anglais** de la liste ci-dessus.
Complete the sentences with the English words from the list above.

1. Je vais chez des amis pour regarder un _____ de football.

2. Son livre est devenu un _____ en moins de deux semaines.

3. On va souvent au casino mais on n'a jamais gagné le _____ .

4. J'adore manger du _____ et des œufs pour le petit déjeuner.

5. Beaucoup de voyageurs prennent des _____ devant la tour Eiffel.

6. Va commander à l'intérieur car il y a trop de monde au _____ .

7. Le _____ devait commencer à 19 heures mais il a commencé à 20 heures.

8. Je vais prendre un _____ au jambon et au fromage, s'il vous plaît.

9. Le _____ s'est bien déroulé mais il était plus long que prévu.

10. Il y a un grand _____ près de la gare.

11. Est-ce que tu as assez de viandes pour le _____ ?

12. Mon compte Instagram a atteint 1000 _____ en quelques mois.

13. L'_____ de la voiture s'est déclenché pendant l'accident.

14. Ta fête d'anniversaire était vraiment _____ .

15. Qu'est-ce que vous prévoyez de faire ce _____ ?

TRANSLATION

1. *I go to a friend's house to watch a soccer match.*

2. *His book became a bestseller in less than two weeks.*

3. *We often go to the casino but we have never won the jackpot.*

4. *I love eating bacon and eggs for breakfast.*

5. *Many travelers take selfies in front of the Eiffel Tower.*

6. *Go order inside because there are too many people at the drive-thru.*

7. *The show was supposed to start at 7 p.m. but it started at 8 p.m.*

8. *I'll have a ham and cheese sandwich, please.*

9. *The meeting went well but it was longer than expected.*

10. *There is a large parking lot near the station.*

11. *Do you have enough meat for the barbecue?*

12. *My Instagram account reached 1000 followers in just a few months.*

13. *The car's airbag was triggered during the accident.*

14. *Your birthday party was really fun.*

15. *What are you planning to do this weekend?*

TOUT CE QU'ON PEUT LIRE
EVERYTHING WE CAN READ

46

AUDIO 46.1

Une affiche nf | *A poster*
Un article nm | *An article*
Une bande dessinée nf | *A comic*
Un blog nm | *A blog*
Une brochure nf | *A brochure*
Un dictionnaire nm | *A dictionary*
Un e-book nm | *An e-book*
Une encyclopédie nf | *An encyclopedia*
Un guide de voyage nm | *A travel guide*
Un journal nm | *A newspaper*

Une lettre nf | *A letter*
Un livre nm | *A book*
Un magazine nm | *A magazine*
Un manuel scolaire nm | *A textbook*
Une notice nf | *Medicine instructions*
Un poème nm | *A poem*
Un prospectus nm | *A flyer*
Une recette nf | *A recipe*
Un roman nm | *A novel*
Un script nm | *A script*

AUDIO 46.2

 Choisissez **le bon mot** pour chaque phrase parmi les mots ci-dessous.
Choose the correct word for each sentence from the words below.

> chapitre – dictionnaire – guide de voyage – journal – lettres – magazines – manuels scolaires – notice – recette – script

1. Chaque soir, je lis un _____ d'un livre avant de dormir.

2. On ne reçoit plus beaucoup de _____ de nos jours.

3. Avant de prendre un médicament, c'est bien de lire la _____ .

4. Je ne trouve pas la _____ de crêpes que j'utilise toujours.

5. Mon père lit le _____ tous les matins en buvant son café.

6. Je ne connais pas ce mot. Je vais regarder sa définition au _____ .

7. On achète toujours des _____ avant de prendre l'avion.

8. Elle oublie toujours ses _____ à l'école.

9. Les acteurs apprennent le _____ par cœur avant de filmer.

10. Je ne trouve pas de _____ sur comment voyager seule.

TRANSLATION

1. *Every evening, I read a chapter of a book before going to sleep.*

2. *We don't get many letters these days.*

3. *Before taking any medication, it is good to read the instructions.*

4. *I can't find the pancake recipe that I always use.*

5. *My father reads the newspaper every morning while drinking his coffee.*

6. *I do not know this word. I'll look up its definition in the dictionary.*

7. *We always buy magazines before boarding a plane.*

8. *She always forgets her textbooks at school.*

9. *The actors learn the script by heart before filming.*

10. *I can't find a travel guide on how to travel alone.*

LES MÉTIERS
JOBS

47

AUDIO 47.1 🔊

Un – Une architecte n | *An architect*
Un acteur – Une actrice n | *An actor*
Un assistant – Une assistante n | *An assistant*
Un agriculteur – Une agricultrice n | *A farmer*
Un – Une astronaute n | *An astronaut*
Un avocat – Une avocate n | *A lawyer*
Un banquier – Une banquière n | *A banker*
Un boucher – Une bouchère n | *A butcher*
Un boulanger – Une boulangère n | *A baker*
Un caissier – Une caissière n | *A cashier*
Un chanteur – Une chanteuse n | *A singer*
Un chauffeur – Une chauffeuse n | *A driver*
Un chirurgien – Une chirurgienne n | *A surgeon*
Un coiffeur – Une coiffeuse n | *A hairdresser*
Un comédien – Une comédienne n | *A comedian*
Un – Une comptable n | *An accountant*
Un conseiller – Une conseillère n | *A consultant*
Un cuisinier – Une cuisinière n | *A cook*
Un danseur – Une danseuse n | *A dancer*
Un directeur – Une directrice n | *A director*
Un – Une dentiste n | *A dentist*
Un docteur – Une docteure n | *A doctor*
Un électricien – Une électricienne n | *An electrician*
Un étudiant – Une étudiante n | *A student*
Un facteur – Une factrice n | *A postman – A postwoman*
Une femme au foyer n | *A housewife*
Un homme au foyer n | *A househusband*
Un fermier – Une fermière n | *A farmer*
Un – Une graphiste n | *A graphic designer*
Un homme d'affaires – Une femme d'affaires n | *A businessman – A businesswoman*
Un infirmier – Une infirmière n | *A nurse*
Un informaticien – Une informaticienne n | *A computer scientist*
Un ingénieur – Une ingénieure n | *An engineer*
Un instituteur – Une institutrice n | *A teacher*
Un – Une journaliste n | *A journalist*
Un – Une libraire n | *A bookseller*

Un mécanicien – Une mécanicienne n | *A mechanic*
Un – Une médecin n | *A doctor*
Un menuisier – Une menuisière n | *A carpenter*
Un musicien – Une musicienne n | *A musician*
Un ouvrier – Une ouvrière n | *A laborer*
Un pâtissier – Une pâtissière n | *A pastry chef*
Un pharmacien – Une pharmacienne n | *A pharmacist*
Un – Une peintre n | *A painter*
Un – Une photographe n | *A photographer*
Un plombier – Une plombière n | *A plumber*
Un policier – Une policière n | *A police officer*
Un – Une pompier n | *A firefighter*
Un professeur – Une professeure n | *A teacher*
Un – Une psychologue n | *A psychologist*
Un – Une secrétaire n | *A secretary*
Un serveur – Une serveuse n | *A waiter*
Un soldat – Une soldate n | *A soldier*
Un vendeur – Une vendeuse n | *A shop assistant*

AUDIO 47.2 ◀))

 Quel est **le métier** des personnes décrites ?
What is the job of the people described?

1. Il travaille dans une banque, il est   .

2. Elle livre le courrier, elle est   .

3. Il scanne les articles à la caisse du magasin, il est   .

4. Elle coupe les cheveux, elle est   .

5. Il soigne les dents, il est   .

6. Elle représente ses clients au tribunal, elle est   .

7. Il s'occupe des patients à l'hôpital, il est   .

8. Elle fait partie des forces de l'ordre, elle est   .

9. Il dessine les plans de maisons, il est   .

10. Elle sert les clients au restaurant, elle est   .

11. Il prépare du pain tous les matins, il est   .

12. Elle joue de la guitare dans un groupe, elle est   .

13. Il va à l'école tous les jours mais il n'est pas professeur, il est

14. Elle joue dans des films et des séries télévisées, elle est

15. Elle aide les clients au magasin de vêtements, elle est   .

TRANSLATION

1. *He works in a bank, he is a banker.*
2. *She delivers the mail, she's a postwoman.*
3. *He scans items at the store checkout, he is a cashier.*
4. *She cuts hair, she is a hairdresser.*
5. *He treats teeth, he is a dentist.*
6. *She represents her clients in court, she is a lawyer.*
7. *He takes care of patients at the hospital, he is a nurse.*
8. *She is part of law enforcement, she is a police officer.*
9. *He draws house plans, he is an architect.*
10. *She serves customers at the restaurant, she is a waitress.*
11. *He prepares bread every morning, he is a baker.*
12. *She plays guitar in a band, she is a musician.*
13. *He goes to school every day but he is not a teacher, he is a student.*
14. *She acts in films and television series, she is an actress.*
15. *She helps customers at the clothing store, she is a saleswoman.*

LES TRANSPORTS
TRANSPORTATIONS

48

AUDIO 48.1 ◀))

Un avion nm | *An airplane*
Un bus nm | *A bus*
Un bateau nm | *A boat*
Une bicyclette nf | *A bike*
Un ferry nm | *A ferry*
Un hélicoptère nm | *A helicopter*
Un camion nm | *A truck*
Un camping-car nm | *A camper van*
Un car nm | *A long-distance bus*
Un métro nm | *A subway*
Une moto nm | *A motorcycle*
Une navette nf | *A shuttle*
Un scooter nm | *A scooter*
Un taxi nm | *A taxi*
Un téléphérique nm | *A cable car*
Un train nm | *A train*
Un train à grande vitesse (TGV) nm |
A high-speed train
Un tramway nm | *A streetcar*
Une trottinette nf | *A scooter*
Une voiture nf | *A car*

Un vélo nm | *A bicycle*
Un vélo électrique nm | *An electric bike*

Aller à pied | *To go by foot*
Aller en voiture | *To go by car*
Aller en train | *To go by train*
Aller en métro | *To go by subway*
Prendre la voiture | *To take the car*
Prendre le train | *To take the train*
Prendre le bus | *To take the bus*

Faire du vélo | *To ride a bike*
Conduire une voiture | *To drive a car*
Piloter un avion | *To fly a plane*
Naviguer un bateau | *To sail a boat*
Attendre le bus | *To wait for the bus*
Monter dans le train | *To get on the train*
Descendre du métro | *To get off the subway*
Faire du covoiturage | *To carpool*
Réserver un taxi | *To book a taxi*
Prendre un vol | *To take a flight*

AUDIO 48.2 ◀))

Ajoutez **le bon mot** ou **groupe de mots** à chaque phrase.
Add the correct word or group of words to each sentence.

à pied – a réservé un taxi – des scooters – deux vélos électriques – en trottinette –
fais du covoiturage – les taxis – monter dans le train – navigue le bateau – prendre l'avion –
prendre le train – prennent le bus – un camping-car – un ferry – un hélicoptère

1. Pour aller en vacances, il faut souvent _____ .

2. Les équipes de secours utilisent _____ pour se rendre
   en montagne.

à pied – **a réservé un taxi** – **des scooters** – **deux vélos électriques** – **en trottinette** –
fais du covoiturage – **les taxis** – **monter dans le train** – **navigue le bateau** – **prendre l'avion** –
prendre le train – **prennent le bus** – **un camping-car** – **un ferry** – **un hélicoptère**

3. Les enfants   tous les jours pour aller à l'école.

4. Il y a   qui relie ces deux îles.

5. On a acheté   pour visiter les États-Unis.

6. En Europe, on peut   à grande vitesse entre certains pays.

7. Ma fille se déplace toujours   .

8. À New York,   sont jaunes.

9. En Italie, beaucoup de touristes louent   .

10. Mes grands-parents ont acheté   .

11. La capitaine   à travers l'océan.

12. Je   avec mes collègues pour aller au travail.

13. On   pour aller à l'aéroport.

14.   peut être difficile pour certains.

15. Je vais à la boulangerie   car elle est proche de chez moi.

TRANSLATION

1. *To go on vacation, you often have to take a plane.*
2. *Rescue teams use a helicopter to get to the mountains.*
3. *The children take the bus every day to go to school.*
4. *There is a ferry that connects these two islands.*
5. *We bought a campervan to visit the United States.*
6. *In Europe, you can take the high-speed train between certain countries.*
7. *My daughter always travels on a scooter.*
8. *In New York, taxis are yellow.*
9. *In Italy, many tourists rent scooters.*
10. *My grandparents bought two electric bikes.*
11. *The captain sails the boat across the ocean.*
12. *I carpool with my colleagues to work.*
13. *We booked a taxi to go to the airport.*
14. *Getting on the train can be difficult for some.*
15. *I go to the bakery on foot because it is close to my house.*

LES ÉMOTIONS

EMOTIONS

49

AUDIO 49.1 🔊

La joie – Le bonheur – *Happiness*

Être content – contente | *To be happy*
Être de bonne humeur | *To be in a good mood*
Être enchanté – enchantée | *To be enchanted*
Être épanoui – épanouie | *To be fulfilled*
Être impatient – impatiente | *To be excited*
Être fier – fière | *To be proud*
Être heureux – heureuse | *To be happy*
Être joyeux – joyeuse | *To be happy*
Être optimiste | *To be optimistic*
Être ravi – ravie | *To be delighted*

AUDIO 49.2 🔊

La tristesse – *Sadness*

Être déçu – déçue | *To be disappointed*
Être démoralisé – démoralisée | *To be demoralized*
Être démotivé – démotivée | *To be demotivated*
Être déprimé – déprimée | *To be depressed*
Être désespéré – désespérée | *To be desperate*
Être dévasté – dévastée | *To be devastated*
Être malheureux – malheureuse | *To be sad*
Être perdu – perdue | *To be lost*
Être pessimiste | *To be pessimistic*
Être triste | *To be sad*

AUDIO 49.3 🔊

La peur – *Fear*

Être angoissé – angoissée | *To be anguished*
Être anxieux – anxieuse | *To be anxious*
Être effrayé – effrayée | *To be scared*
Être inquiet – inquiète | *To be worried*
Être nerveux – nerveuse | *To be nervous*
Être paniqué – paniquée | *To be panicked*

Être stressé – stressée | *To be stressed*
Être terrifié – terrifiée | *To be terrified*
Être terrorisé – terrorisée | *To be terrorized*

AUDIO 49.4 ◄))

L'amour – *Love*

Être amoureux – amoureuse | *To be in love*
Être fou – folle de | *To be crazy about*
Être passionné – passionnée | *To be passionate*

AUDIO 49.5 ◄))

La colère – *Anger*

Être de mauvaise humeur | *To be in a bad mood*
Être dégoûté – dégoûtée | *To be disgusted*
Être écœuré – écœurée | *To be disgusted*
Être en colère | *To be angry*
Être énervé – énervée | *To be mad*
Être fâché – fâchée | *To be angry*
Être frustré – frustrée | *To be frustrated*
Être furieux – furieuse | *To be furious*
Être hors de soi | *To be out of oneself*
Être mécontent – mécontente | *To be dissatisfied*

AUDIO 49.6 ◄))

La fatigue – *Tiredness*

Être crevé – crevée | *To be tired*
Être vidé – vidée | *To be drained*
Être débordé – débordée | *To be overwhelmed*
Être découragé – découragée | *To be discouraged*
Être épuisé – épuisée | *To be exhausted*
Être fatigué – fatiguée | *To be tired*

AUDIO 49.7 ◄))

La honte – *Shame*

Être désolé – désolée | *To be sorry*
Être gêné – gênée | *To be embarrassed*
Être honteux – honteuse | *To be ashamed*

Choisissez **le bon adjectif** pour chaque phrase.
Choose the correct adjective for each sentence.

1. **débordé – désolé** – Je suis _____ de ne pas avoir pu venir à ton mariage.

2. **énervé – fière** – Il était _____ mais je ne sais pas pourquoi.

3. **inquiets – honteux** – Mes parents sont _____ car ils n'ont pas de nouvelles de mon frère.

4. **heureux – terrorisés** – On est _____ d'avoir fini nos études.

5. **fatiguée – contente** – Tu es _____ car tu n'as pas assez dormi.

6. **pessimiste – gênée** – Elle est toujours _____ de parler en public.

7. **nerveux – fier** – Tu peux être _____ de toi.

8. **impatient – malheureux** – Il est _____ depuis son divorce.

9. **fatigués – amoureux** – Ils sont follement _____ l'un de l'autre.

10. **nerveux – perdu** – Le patient est _____ avant son examen.

11. **épanouie – crevée** – C'est bien de te voir _____ .

12. **vidés – déçus** – Ils étaient _____ que tu ne sois pas venu.

13. **joyeux – furieux** – Son père était _____ quand il a eu son accident.

14. **impatient – triste** – Le train va bientôt arriver. Ne sois pas aussi _____ .

15. **découragés – fatigués** – Les élèves sont _____ après avoir eu de mauvaises notes.

TRANSLATION

1. *I'm sorry I couldn't come to your wedding.*

2. *He was angry but I don't know why.*

3. *My parents are worried because they have not heard from my brother.*

4. *We are happy to have finished our studies.*

5. *You're tired because you didn't get enough sleep.*

6. *She is always embarrassed to speak in public.*

7. *You can be proud of yourself.*

8. *He has been unhappy since his divorce.*

9. *They are madly in love with each other.*

10. *The patient is nervous before his exam.*

11. *It's good to see you fulfilled.*

12. *They were disappointed that you didn't come.*

13. *His father was furious when he had his accident.*

14. *The train will arrive soon. Don't be so impatient.*

15. *Students become discouraged after getting poor grades.*

LA FAMILLE
FAMILY

50

La famille nf | *Family*

Les enfants nm | *The children*
Les parents nm | *The parents*

Un mari nm | *A husband*
Une femme nf | *A wife*
Un père nm | *A father*
Une mère nf | *A mother*
Un fils nm | *A son*
Une fille nf | *A daughter*
Un frère nm | *A brother*
Une sœur nf | *A sister*

L'aîné nm | *The oldest*
L'aînée nf | *The oldest*
Le cadet nm | *The youngest*
La cadette nf | *The youngest*

Des jumeaux nm | *Twins*
Des jumelles nf | *Twins*
Des triplés nm | *Triplets*

Un parrain nm | *A godfather*
Une marraine nf | *A godmother*
Un filleul nm | *A godson*
Une filleule nf | *A goddaughter*

Un cousin nm | *A cousin*
Une cousine nf | *A cousin*
Un oncle nm | *An uncle*
Une tante nf | *An aunt*
Un neveu nm | *A nephew*
Une nièce nf | *A niece*

Un grand-père nm | *A grandfather*
Une grand-mère nf | *A grandmother*
Les grands-parents nm | *The grandparents*
Les petits-enfants nm | *The grandchildren*
Un petit-fils nm | *A grandson*
Une petite-fille nf | *A granddaughter*

Un demi-frère nm | *A half-brother*
Une demi-sœur nf | *A half-sister*

Un beau-fils nm | *A son-in-law – A stepson*
Une belle-fille nf | *A daughter-in-law – A stepdaughter*
Un beau-frère nm | *A brother-in-law – A stepbrother*
Une belle-sœur nf | *A sister-in-law – A stepsister*
Un beau-père nm | *A father-in-law – A stepfather*
Une belle-mère nf | *A mother-in-law – A stepmother*
Les beaux-parents nm | *The parents-in-law – Stepparents*

Les proches nm | *Relatives*

Beau and belle are used to refer to in-law and step-. Usually, the context will tell you more about who is who.

Complétez les phrases avec **le vocabulaire** ci-dessus.
Complete the sentences with the vocabulary above.

1. C'est le fils de ma sœur, c'est mon   .

2. Je suis la marraine du fils de mes amis, c'est mon   .

3. C'est la mère de mon père, c'est ma   .

4. C'est le mari de ma mère mais ce n'est pas mon père, c'est mon   .

5. C'est la fille de ma grand-mère mais ce n'est pas ma mère, c'est ma   .

6. C'est la personne que j'ai épousée, c'est mon   .

7. Je suis le plus âgé de mes frères et sœurs, je suis l'   .

8. Mes frères sont nés le même jour, ce sont des   .

9. C'est la fille de la sœur de mon mari, c'est ma   .

10. Je suis la filleule de la meilleure amie de ma mère, c'est ma   .

11. C'est le fils de mon fils, c'est mon   .

12. Je suis la plus jeune de mes frères et sœurs, je suis la   .

13. C'est la fille de ma tante, c'est ma   .

14. Ce sont toutes les personnes de ma famille, ce sont mes   .

15. C'est le fils de ma mère et de mon beau-père, c'est mon   .

TRANSLATION

1. *He's my sister's son, he's my nephew.*
2. *I am the godmother of my friends' son, he is my godson.*
3. *She's my father's mother, she's my grandmother.*
4. *He's my mother's husband but he's not my father, he's my stepfather.*
5. *She's my grandmother's daughter but she's not my mother, she's my aunt.*
6. *This is the person I married, this is my husband.*

7. *I am the oldest of my siblings, I am the eldest.*

8. *My brothers were born on the same day, they are twins.*

9. *She's my husband's sister's daughter, she's my niece.*

10. *I am the goddaughter of my mother's best friend, she is my godmother.*

11. *He's my son's son, he's my grandson.*

12. *I am the youngest of my siblings, I am the youngest.*

13. *She's my aunt's daughter, she's my cousin.*

14. *These are all the people in my family, these are my loved ones.*

15. *He's the son of my mother and my stepfather, he's my half-brother.*

ANSWER KEY

CHAPTER 1

1. Je dors dans ma **chambre**.
2. Je prépare mes repas dans la **cuisine**.
3. Je fais ma lessive dans la **buanderie**.
4. Je me lave dans la **salle de bain**.
5. Je range le balai dans le **débarras**.
6. Je travaille dans mon **bureau**.
7. Quand mes amis me rendent visite, ils dorment dans la **chambre d'amis**.
8. Le soir, je gare ma voiture dans le **garage**.
9. Mes habits sont rangés dans le **dressing**.
10. Mes bouteilles de vin sont à la **cave**.
11. Je regarde la télévision dans le **salon**.
12. Les enfants jouent dans la **salle de jeux**.
13. La pièce que je préfère chez moi : **le salon**
14. La pièce que j'aime le moins chez moi : **la cuisine**
15. La pièce que j'aimerais avoir chez moi : **une véranda**

CHAPTER 2

1. Quelle est votre **pointure** ?
2. J'**ai commandé** des vêtements en ligne.
3. Mets ton **gilet** si tu as froid.
4. On **s'habille** toujours avant de prendre notre petit déjeuner.
5. Mes **chaussures** sont pleines de boue.
6. Cette **robe** te va très bien.
7. Tu as pris tes **baskets** pour courir ?
8. C'est bien de porter des **tongs** à la piscine.
9. Il faut toujours **essayer** avant d'acheter.
10. Ce pantalon est mal **taillé**.
11. Je dois faire réparer mes **bottes** pour l'hiver.
12. On va **faire du shopping** ce week-end.
13. Ce manteau est trop **petit** pour toi.
14. Est-ce que vous avez la **taille** au-dessus ?
15. Je pense **acheter** un nouveau pull pour mes vacances.

CHAPTER 3

1. vidéo – ~~lien~~ – Est-ce que tu as vu la **vidéo** que je viens de publier ?
2. ~~tendance~~ – **demande d'ami** – Tu n'as pas reçu ma **demande d'ami** ?
3. ~~abonné~~ – **émoji** – Elle ajoute toujours un **émoji** à la fin de ses phrases.
4. abonnés – ~~groupes~~ – Son compte Instagram a 2000 **abonnés**.
5. ~~compte~~ – **chaîne** – Je n'ai jamais regardé sa **chaîne** YouTube.
6. lien – ~~nom d'utilisateur~~ – L'auteur a partagé le **lien** de son livre dans sa story.
7. ~~bloqué~~ – **en ligne** – Je vois qu'il est **en ligne** mais il ne me répond pas.
8. ~~commentaire~~ – **photo de profil** – Elle veut changer sa **photo de profil** mais elle ne trouve pas de belle photo.
9. nom d'utilisateur – ~~réseau social~~ – Quel est ton **nom d'utilisateur** ?
10. applications – ~~groupe~~ – Combien d'**applications** est-ce que vous utilisez ?
11. ~~chaîne~~ – **compte** – Mon **compte** est bloqué mais je ne sais pas pourquoi.
12. commentaires – ~~tendances~~ – On aime lire les **commentaires** en-dessous de nos photos.
13. groupes – ~~comptes~~ – Ma mère est dans plusieurs **groupes** Facebook.
14. ~~vidéo~~ – **fil d'actualité** – Il n'y a rien de nouveau sur mon **fil d'actualité**.
15. discute – ~~navigue~~ – Je **discute** avec beaucoup de gens en ligne.

CHAPTER 4

1. Je dois être à l'**aéroport** dans deux heures pour prendre mon avion.
2. Le criminel sera jugé au **tribunal**.
3. Elle fait toujours ses courses au **supermarché/centre commercial** du coin.
4. Ils viennent d'acheter un appartement tout en haut de ce **gratte-ciel**.
5. Est-ce que tu peux aller à la **pharmacie** pour aller chercher ses médicaments ?
6. J'aime habiter à côté d'une **boulangerie** car ma maison sent toujours le pain.
7. La **boucherie** a des promotions sur le blanc de poulet.
8. Les enfants vont à la **bibliothèque** pour lire des histoires.
9. Nous avons passé nos vacances dans un **hôtel** près de la plage.
10. Tu dois aller chercher ton colis au **bureau de poste** aujourd'hui.
11. Elle doit s'arrêter à la **station d'essence** car sa voiture n'a plus d'essence.
12. Mon père travaille dans une **usine** de papier.
13. J'ai commandé un énorme beaucoup de roses chez le **fleuriste**.
14. On peut trouver de bonnes affaires au **magasin de seconde main**.
15. Je vais boire un verre avec mon mari au **café** après le travail.

CHAPTER 5

1. Je m'appelle Dylane.

   My name is Dylane.

2. J'ai 36 ans.

   I am 36 years old.

3. Mon anniversaire est le 19 novembre.

   My birthday is November 19th.

4. J'habite à Paris, en France.

   I live in Paris in France.

5. Je suis professeure de français.

   I am a French teacher.

6. J'ai quatre frères mais je n'ai pas de sœur.

   I have four brothers but I don't have a sister.

7. J'ai les cheveux blonds.

   I have blond hair.

8. Je mesure 1 mètre 64.

   I am 1 meter 64 tall.

9. Je me lève à 7 heures tous les matins.

   I get up at 7 a.m. every morning.

10. Pendant mon temps libre, j'aime jouer aux jeux vidéo.

    In my free time, I like to play video games.

11. Mon fruit préféré est la banane.

    My favorite fruit is banana.

12. Ma boisson préférée est le café.

    My favorite drink is coffee.

13. Oui, j'ai un chien.

    Yes, I have a dog.

14. Je parle français et anglais.

    I speak French and English.

15. Je me couche tous les soirs à 22 heures.

    I go to bed every night at 10 p.m.

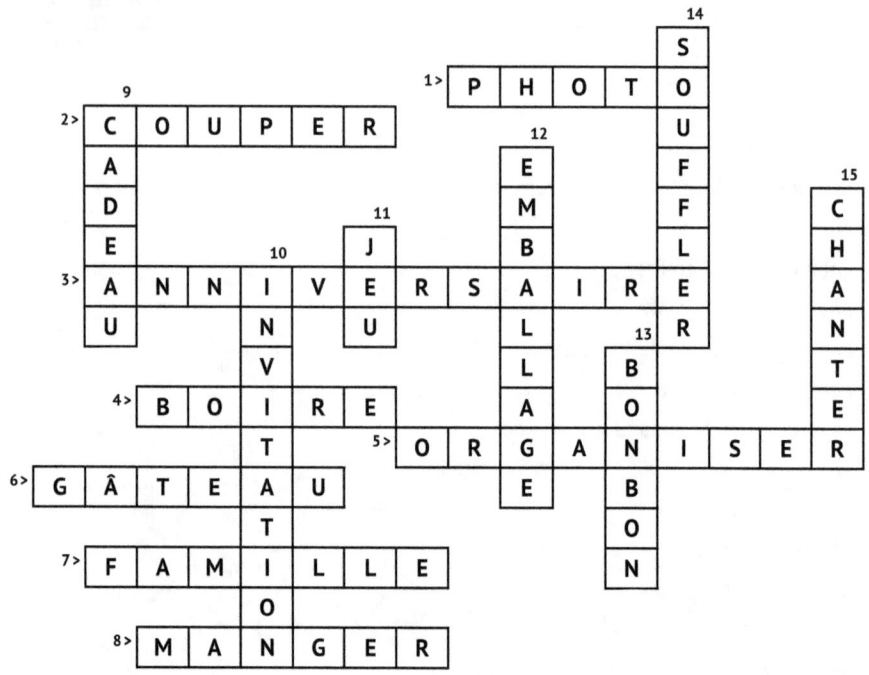

CHAPTER 6

CHAPTER 7

1. La neige est **blanche**.
2. Les citrons sont **jaunes**.
3. Le drapeau français est **bleu**, **blanc** et **rouge**.
4. L'habit du Père Noël est **rouge** et **blanc**.
5. Il pleut, le ciel est **gris**.
6. Le mur devant moi est **blanc**.
7. Mon pull est **beige**.
8. Ma bouteille d'eau est **rose**.
9. La couverture sur mon lit est **bleue**.
10. Mon canapé est **gris**.

CHAPTER 8

1. Je n'ai plus rien de propre. Je dois **faire la lessive**.
2. Est-ce que tu **es au courant** de la nouvelle ?
3. Elle a reçu les résultats de sa prise de sang. Elle **est en bonne santé**.
4. Il **fait des progrès** avec son nouveau professeur.
5. Je n'ai pas bu d'eau aujourd'hui. J'**ai soif**.
6. Est-ce que tu as un médicament pour la migraine ? J'**ai mal à la tête**.
7. **Fais attention** de ne pas tomber en descendant de l'échelle.
8. Je dois aller chez le dentiste aujourd'hui car j'**ai mal aux dents**.
9. On essaye de **faire une promenade** tous les soirs après le dîner.
10. Il n'a pas de voiture donc il **va à pied** au travail.
11. Les enfants **font leurs devoirs** en rentrant de l'école.
12. Je **fais du sport** 5 fois par semaine au minimum.
13. Il **a de la chance** d'avoir une belle maison.
14. Les températures ont atteint 40 degrés. Il **fait chaud** !
15. Je me suis levé en retard, je **suis en retard**.

CHAPTER 9

1. an – ~~en~~ – Mon fils va avoir un **an** dans une semaine.
2. ~~laid~~ – lait – Est-ce que tu peux acheter du **lait** au magasin avant de rentrer ?
3. ~~hockey~~ – hoquet – Il joue au **hockey** 3 fois par semaine depuis qu'il est petit.
4. ~~Il~~ – Ils – **Ils** ont reçu mon message mais ils ne m'ont pas répondu.
5. dans – ~~dent~~ – Mon téléphone est resté **dans** la voiture.
6. lac – ~~laque~~ – Le **lac** est presque vide à cause de la sécheresse.
7. ~~faim~~ – fin – La **fin** du film était tellement triste !
8. ~~Sang~~ – Sans – **Sans** toi je ne suis rien.
9. ~~amendes~~ – amandes – Je préfère le lait d'**amandes**.
10. bout – ~~boue~~ – Est-ce que tu veux un **bout** de gâteau ?
11. ~~comptant~~ – content – Il était vraiment **content** de te voir.
12. cou – ~~coup~~ – Elle s'est fail mal au **cou** en jouant au basket.
13. ~~signes~~ – cygnes – Il y a des **cygnes** autour du lac.
14. ~~la~~ – là – Tu seras **là** ce soir ?
15. mai – ~~mais~~ – Ma fille est née au mois de **mai**.

CHAPTER 10

1. **V** – La tour Eiffel est située à Paris.
2. **V** – La Terre est la troisième planète du système solaire.
3. **F** – Le Japon est connu pour sa production de fromage. (de voitures)
4. **V** – Le Titanic a coulé en 1912.
5. **F** – La capitale de l'Italie est Madrid. (Rome)
6. **V** – Les chiens sont des mammifères.
7. **V** – L'eau gèle à 0 degrés Celsius.
8. **F** – La Grande Muraille de Chine est visible depuis la Lune.
9. **V** – Les chats ont quatre pattes.
10. **V** – Les abeilles produisent du miel.
11. **V** – Le mont Everest est le plus haut sommet du monde.
12. **F** – Les serpents sont des animaux à sang chaud. (à sang froid)
13. **F** – La capitale de la France est Berlin. (Paris)
14. **V** – Le soleil se lève à l'est et se couche à l'ouest.
15. **F** – Les pingouins peuvent voler.
16. **V** – L'arc-en-ciel a sept couleurs distinctes.
17. **V** – Les éléphants sont les plus gros mammifères terrestres.
18. **F** – Le pôle Nord est le point le plus au sud de la Terre. (le plus au nord)
19. **V** – La Lune tourne autour de la Terre.
20. **F** – Les dauphins sont des poissons. (des mammifères)

CHAPTER 11

1. Mon anniversaire est en **novembre**.
2. Mon jour préféré est le **jeudi**.
3. Mon prochain rendez-vous est un **mercredi**.
4. Ma saison préférée est **l'hiver**.
5. Noël est en **décembre** et en **hiver**.
6. Les feuilles changent de couleurs en **automne**.
7. Les enfants vont à l'école du **lundi** au **vendredi**.
8. On partira en vacances en **septembre**.
9. Aujourd'hui, on est **vendredi**.
10. **Dimanche** est un jour de repos pour beaucoup de monde.
11. **Lundi** est le premier jour de la semaine.

12. La rentrée scolaire est en **septembre**.

13. Le mois le plus court de l'année est le mois de **février**.

14. Halloween est célébrée en **octobre**.

15. Beaucoup d'élèves sont en vacances en **juillet** et en **août**.

CHAPTER 12

1. Un carré en 3D est un **cube.**

2. Un triangle en 3D est une **pyramide.**

3. Un cercle en 3D est une **sphère.**

4. Un **carré** a quatre côtés égaux.

5. Un **rectangle** a deux côtés longs et deux côtés courts.

6. Un **triangle** est une forme avec trois côtés.

7. Un **cercle** est une forme ronde sans côtés.

8. Un **hexagone** a six côtés égaux.

9. Un **croissant** est en forme de lune.

10. Un **cœur** est une forme qui représente l'amour.

CHAPTER 13

1. **/** – J'étudie le français.

2. **M** – Je me lève tôt.

3. **M S** – Je me brosse les dents.

4. **S** – Je prends une douche ou un bain.

5. **M A S** – Je passe du temps sur mon téléphone.

6. **M** – Je prends mon petit déjeuner.

7. **M** – Je me prépare pour la journée.

8. **A S** – Je mets mon pyjama.

9. **S** – Je mets mon réveil pour le lendemain matin.

10. **A S** – Je fais du sport.

11. **S** – Je prépare le dîner.

12. **A** – Je rentre du travail ou de l'école.

13. **M A** – Je fais les courses.

14. **S** – Je prépare mes affaires pour le lendemain.

15. **M** – Je vérifie mes emails.

CHAPTER 14

1. ~~cerveau~~ – **dos** – Il s'est fait mal au **dos** en portant cette boîte lourde.
2. **poignet** – ~~cheville~~ – Elle a beaucoup trop de bracelets au **poignet**.
3. ~~auriculaire~~ – annulaire – On porte son alliance à l'**annulaire**.
4. **reins** – ~~estomac~~ – Les **reins** filtrent les toxines du corps.
5. ~~phalange~~ – vessie – Elle a une petite **vessie**. Elle doit toujours aller aux toilettes.
6. **coudes** – ~~organes~~ – Ne mets pas tes **coudes** sur la table.
7. **mollet** – ~~cerveau~~ – J'ai souvent des crampes au **mollet**.
8. ~~ventre~~ – **épaule** – Son **épaule** est douloureuse depuis son match de tennis.
9. ~~genoux~~ – ongles – Elle a toujours du vernis sur ses **ongles**.
10. **poitrine** – cuisse – Il faut aller à l'hôpital si on a mal à la **poitrine**.

CHAPTER 15

1. **Remplissez** une casserole d'eau. Faites **bouillir** l'eau et **ajoutez** les nouilles. Faites **cuire** les nouilles selon les instructions du paquet.
2. **Hachez** l'ail et ajoutez-le dans une poêle avec une cuillère à soupe d'huile. Faites **sauter** à feu doux pendant environ deux minutes ou jusqu'à ce que l'ail soit doré. **Ajoutez** le gingembre et faites **revenir** une minute de plus.
3. **Ajoutez** tous les ingrédients restants de la sauce et **fouettez** pour atteindre la consistance souhaitée.
4. **Goûtez** et ajoutez plus de sauce soja ou de sauce piquante selon vos goûts.
5. **Égouttez** les nouilles et ajoutez plus ou moins la moitié de la sauce aux nouilles cuites et **mélangez**.
6. **Servez** avec des cacahuètes, des brocolis, des carottes, des oignons verts et **dégustez** !

CHAPTER 16

1. ~~diplomes~~ – **diplômes** – Les élèves ont reçu leurs **diplômes** à la fin de l'année scolaire.
2. ~~vacance~~ – vacances – Qu'est-ce que tu as de prévu en **vacances** ?
3. **Apparemment** – ~~Apparement~~ – **Apparemment**, il vient de demander le divorce.
4. **circonstances** – ~~circonstences~~ – Je ne connais pas les **circonstances** de l'accident.
5. ~~consience~~ – conscience – Il a mauvaise **conscience** après ce qu'il a dit.
6. **recommander** – ~~recommender~~ – Est-ce que tu peux me **recommander** un bon restaurant ?
7. **immédiate** – ~~imédiate~~ – J'ai besoin d'une réponse **immédiate**.

8. lavande – ~~lavende~~ – On a pris des photos devant ce champ de **lavande**.
9. poireaux – ~~porreaux~~ – Est-ce que tu as une bonne recette de soupe aux **poireaux** ?
10. ~~ognions~~ – oignons – Les **oignons** me font toujours pleurer.
11. ~~documantaire~~ – documentaire – Ce **documentaire** est un succès.
12. ~~passport~~ – passeport – N'oublie pas de prendre ton **passeport**.
13. applaudissements – ~~aplaudissements~~ – Elle a reçu beaucoup d'**applaudissements** après son concert.
14. ~~boullir~~ – bouillir – Faites **bouillir** l'eau avant d'y mettre les pâtes.
15. papillons – ~~pappillons~~ – Il y a des **papillons** sur les fleurs.

CHAPTER 17

1. Ce gâteau est tellement **bon** !
   Ce gâteau est tellement **mauvais** !
2. Fais attention, l'eau du bain est très **chaude**.
   Fais attention, l'eau du bain est très **froide**.
3. Son mari a toujours été **fidèle**.
   Son mari a toujours été **infidèle**.
4. Le magasin est déjà **ouvert**.
   Le magasin est déjà **fermé**.
5. Ce puzzle est trop **difficile** pour moi.
   Ce puzzle est trop **facile** pour moi.
6. Il a toujours été **gentil** avec mes parents.
   Il a toujours été **méchant** avec mes parents.
7. C'est le pont le plus **long** du pays.
   C'est le pont le plus **court** du pays.
8. Tous les ingrédients de ce produit sont **artificiels**.
   Tous les ingrédients de ce produit sont **naturels**.
9. Est-ce que tu es **occupé** ce samedi ?
   Est-ce que tu es **libre** ce samedi ?
10. Sa maison est toujours **organisée**.
    Sa maison est toujours **désorganisée**.
11. Je pense que cette chemise est **sale**.
    Je pense que cette chemise est **propre**.
12. L'herbe était **humide** ce matin.
    L'herbe était **sèche** ce matin.

13. Le plat est assez **salé** pour moi.

Le plat est assez **sucré** pour moi.

14. Cet outil est **utile** pour ce projet.

Cet outil est **inutile** pour ce projet.

15. Le réservoir de ma voiture est **plein**.

Le réservoir de ma voiture est **vide**.

CHAPTER 18

1. Pour faire du café, j'utilise la **cafetière**.
2. Pour cuire un gâteau, j'utilise le **four**.
3. Pour nettoyer la vaisselle, j'utilise le **lave-vaisselle**.
4. Pour conserver les aliments, je les mets au **réfrigérateur**.
5. Pour congeler mes plats, je les mets au **congélateur**.
6. Pour faire du thé, j'utilise la **théière**.
7. Pour griller du pain, j'utilise le **grille-pain**.
8. Pour réchauffer un plat, j'utilise un **(four à) micro-ondes**.
9. Pour éplucher les carottes, j'utilise un **éplucheur**.
10. Pour ouvrir une boîte de conserve, j'utilise un **ouvre-boîtes**.

CHAPTER 19

1. **F** – Je mesure plus d'un mètre soixante.
2. **V** – Je prends toujours un petit déjeuner.
3. **V** – Je parle deux langues couramment.
4. **F** – Je préfère regarder un film plutôt qu'une série télévisée.
5. **F** – Je fais toujours mon ménage le dimanche.
6. **V** – Je travaille à domicile.
7. **F** – Je suis abonné(e) à un journal ou un magazine.
8. **V** – Je porte des lunettes.
9. **F** – Je mange des légumes à chaque repas.
10. **V** – Je lis au moins un livre par mois.
11. **V** – J'aime manger au restaurant de temps en temps.
12. **F** – Je préfère me lever tard.
13. **V** – Je suis introverti(e) plutôt qu'extraverti(e).
14. **V** – Je préfère les vacances à la montagne plutôt qu'à la plage.

15. **F** – Je conduis ma voiture tous les jours.
16. **F** – Je vais souvent au cinéma pour voir un film.
17. **F** – Je fais mes courses en ligne plutôt qu'en magasin.
18. **F** – J'étudie le français tous les jours.
19. **V** – J'aime recevoir mes amis chez moi.
20. **F** – Je sais jouer de la guitare.

CHAPTER 20

Dany a commencé la journée avec un **bon** petit déjeuner. Il a une journée **chargée** au bureau aujourd'hui avec une réunion et une conférence. La réunion va sûrement être **stressante** car il y a beaucoup de problèmes à régler. La conférence, elle, va certainement être **ennuyante**.

Quand Dany arrive au bureau, il se sent tout de suite **frustré**. Son ordinateur est **en panne** et personne ne peut venir le réparer. Toute l'équipe informatique est **occupée** ce matin. Il peut utiliser son ordinateur portable mais il est très **lent**. Cela va lui prendre un temps **interminable** de préparer sa réunion. Il est 10 heures et Dany est déjà **fatigué**. La journée va être **longue**.

Après sa réunion, Dany va prendre son déjeuner. La réunion a été **éprouvante**. Il est **content** qu'elle soit finie ! À 14 heures, il doit aller à une conférence pour parler du **dernier** trimestre de l'année. Il est **impatient** de rentrer chez lui.

CHAPTER 21

1. **niche** – Mon **chien** joue dans le jardin avec sa balle.
2. **port** – J'ai **trop** de pommes de terre dans mon assiette.
3. **mon** – Est-ce que tu peux épeler ton **nom** ?
4. **ami** – On a réservé un hôtel pour le mois de **mai**.
5. **soif** – Mes parents ont visité cette ville plusieurs **fois** quand ils étaient jeunes.
6. **ride** – Qu'est-ce que tu veux **dire** ?
7. **obéir** – Ce n'est pas bon de **boire** trop d'alcool.
8. **coupe** – Il s'est coupé le **pouce** en travaillant dans le jardin.
9. **neige** – C'est une idée de **génie** !
10. **charme** – Fais attention à la **marche**.
11. **rose** – Il faut **oser** faire ce qu'on veut dans la vie.
12. **stop** – On a beaucoup de plantes en **pots** sur notre terrasse.

13. **suer** – Les **rues** de la capitale sont bondées.
14. **rois** – Qu'est-ce que tu fais ce **soir** ?
15. **lime** – Ce **miel** est délicieux !

CHAPTER 22

1. Ce **paquet de** chips est déjà ouvert.
2. Le **pot de** confiture est sur la table si tu en veux.
3. Je mange deux **tranches de** pain tous les matins.
4. On a mangé une **tablette de** chocolat devant la télévision.
5. Est-ce que tu veux un **morceau de** gâteau ?
6. Il boit une **canette/bouteille d'**eau pétillante avec son dîner.
7. La recette dit d'ajouter deux **cuillères** à café de sucre.
8. 1000 grammes = 1 **kilo**
9. 1000 kilos = 1 **tonne**
10. 1000 millilitres = 1 **litre**

CHAPTER 23

1. Pour rester propre, c'est important de **se laver** chaque jour.
2. Le matin, je **m'habille** avant de sortir de ma chambre.
3. Je **me brosse** les cheveux et les dents.
4. Le soir, j'aime prendre un **bain** pour me détendre.
5. Après mon bain, je mets du **déodorant** pour ne pas sentir la transpiration.
6. Quand je rentre chez moi, je **me déshabille** et je me mets en pyjama.
7. Avant de me coucher, je **me démaquille** avec un produit doux.
8. Après le shampoing, j'utilise de l'**après-shampoing** pour démêler mes cheveux.
9. Beaucoup d'hommes **se rasent** avant d'aller au bureau.
10. Je préfère me laver avec du **savon** plutôt qu'avec du gel douche.
11. Je **me maquille** presque tous les jours.
12. C'est bien d'utiliser du **fil dentaire** avant de se laver les dents.
13. Ma **brosse à dents électrique** n'a plus de batterie.
14. Est-ce que tu as vu mon **rasoir** ?
15. Je **sens bon** après un bain moussant.

CHAPTER 24

1. pousser – ~~tailler~~ – Le fertilisant aide à faire **pousser** les légumes.
2. chaise longue – ~~chaise d'extérieur~~ – Ma mère adore s'allonger sur cette **chaise longue**.
3. arroser – ~~cultiver~~ – Il faut **arroser** les plantes quand il fait trop chaud.
4. ~~tondeuse~~ – clôture – Mon jardin est fermé par une **clôture**.
5. ~~faire pousser~~ – jardiner – J'adore **jardiner** quand j'ai du temps libre.
6. fleurs – ~~potagers~~ – Au printemps, certaines **fleurs** commencent à éclore.
7. ~~a récolté~~ – a semé – On **a semé** les graines il y a un mois mais rien ne pousse.
8. ~~hamac~~ – parasol – On a acheté **un parasol** pour avoir de l'ombre quand on est assis à la table d'extérieur.
9. ~~creuser~~ – récolter – Il est temps de **récolter** les pommes avant que les oiseaux ne les mangent.
10. ~~jardin~~ – potager – J'ai commencé un **potager** avec des carottes, des courgettes et des pommes de terre.
11. ~~récolte~~ – tond – Le voisin **tond** sa pelouse tous les samedis matin.
12. hamac – ~~balançoire~~ – Quand j'aurai un jardin, j'aurai un **hamac** pour faire des siestes.
13. ~~arrose~~ – cultive – Le fermier **cultive** ce champ depuis des années.
14. serre – ~~haie~~ – La **serre** permet de faire pousser des fleurs toute l'année.
15. taille – ~~tond~~ – Le jardinier **taille** les buissons.

CHAPTER 25

1. J'aime **promener Beefy**.
   I like walking Beefy.
2. J'aime **les brocolis**.
   I like broccoli.
3. J'aime **dormir tard**.
   I like to sleep late.
4. J'aime **lire dans mon lit**.
   I like to read in bed.
5. J'aime **faire du sport**.
   I like to play sports.
6. Je n'aime pas **être en retard**.
   I don't like being late.
7. Je n'aime pas **courir**.
   I don't like running.
8. Je n'aime pas **les champignons**.
   I don't like mushrooms.
9. Je n'aime pas **parler en public**.
   I don't like speaking in public.
10. Je n'aime pas **la pluie**.
    I don't like the rain.

CHAPTER 26

1.   Le **sirop d'érable** vient de l'érable.
2.   Les **citrons** poussent sur le citronnier.
3.   Les **cerises** poussent sur le cerisier.
4.   Les **pommes** poussent sur le pommier.
5.   Les **fraises** poussent sur le fraisier.
6.   Les **avocats** poussent sur l'avocatier.
7.   Les **olives** poussent sur l'olivier.
8.   Les **oranges** poussent sur l'oranger.
9.   Les **prunes** poussent sur le prunier.
10. Les **bananes** poussent sur le bananier.
11. Les **mangues** poussent sur le manguier.
12. Les **framboises** poussent sur le framboisier.

CHAPTER 27

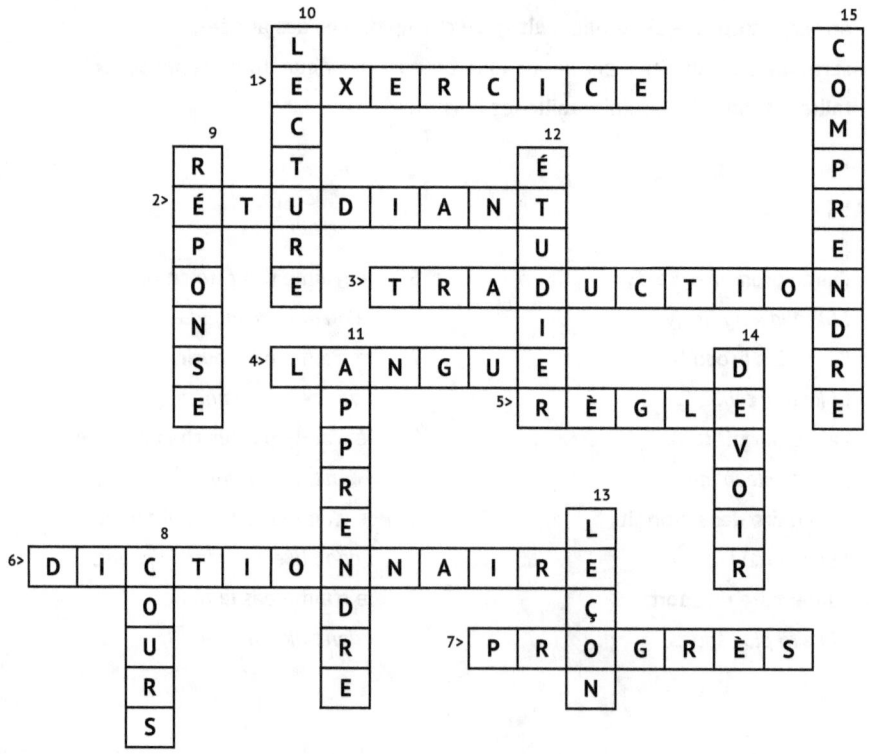

CHAPTER 28

1. La **coiffeuse** a coupé **mes cheveux** beaucoup trop **courts**.
2. Une **coloration** abîme **les cheveux**.
3. Cette **coupe de cheveux** ne te va pas très **bien**.
4. Je lis toujours plusieurs **magazines** quand je suis chez le coiffeur.
5. Les cheveux **roux** sont assez rares.
6. Elle a demandé au coiffeur de ne couper que les **pointes**.
7. Le coiffeur utilise des **ciseaux** pour couper les cheveux.
8. Le coiffeur va me couper les cheveux d'abord, puis me faire un **brushing**.
9. Elle coupe les cheveux de son mari avec un **rasoir électrique**.
10. J'ai demandé une **frange** mais je le regrette déjà.

CHAPTER 29

1. ~~propre~~ – ~~gâté~~ – peureux – ~~content~~
   Mon chat est **peureux** depuis qu'il est petit. Il se cache toujours quand j'ai des invités.
2. dos – ~~dents~~ – ~~yeux~~ – ~~queue~~
   Le vétérinaire examine le **dos** du chien vu qu'il a du mal à marcher.
3. ~~miaule~~ – ~~joue~~ – ~~caresse~~ – ronronne
   Son chat **ronronne** quand il mange.
4. ~~croquettes~~ – poils – ~~pattes~~ – ~~jouets~~
   Le chat a commencé à perdre ses **poils**.
5. ~~manger~~ – ~~changer~~ – ~~jouer~~ – promener
   On essaye de **promener** nos chiens 2 fois par jour.
6. chiens guides – ~~chiots~~ – ~~chiens d'assistance~~ – ~~chats~~
   Les **chiens guides** sont importants pour les personnes malvoyantes.
7. ~~museau~~ – queue – ~~moustache~~ – ~~truffe~~
   Un chien remue la **queue** quand il est content.
8. pâtée – ~~croquette~~ – ~~litière~~ – ~~race~~
   Mon chien et mon chat mangent de la **pâtée** car ils n'ont plus de dents.
9. ~~yeux~~ – pattes – ~~dents~~ – ~~harnais~~
   C'est bien de nettoyer les **pattes** du chien après une promenade.
10. ~~dresser~~ – caresser – ~~promener~~ – ~~aboyer~~
    Les enfants du quartier veulent toujours **caresser** mon chien.
11. gâtés – ~~peureux~~ – ~~propres~~ – ~~affectueux~~
    Ses animaux sont **gâtés**. Ils ne manquent de rien.

12. ~~chien~~ – chiot – ~~éleveur~~ – ~~chat~~

Un **chiot** demande beaucoup d'attention jusqu'à l'âge adulte.

13. ~~laisse~~ – ~~litière~~ – ~~balle~~ – harnais

Notre chien a tellement grandi qu'il a besoin d'un nouveau **harnais**.

14. ~~fourrure~~ – ~~race~~ – litière – ~~croquette~~

Il faut changer la **litière** régulièrement pour qu'elle ne sente pas.

15. miaule – ~~aboie~~ – ~~joue~~ – ~~dresse~~

Mon chat **miaule** toujours pour me réveiller le matin.

CHAPTER 30

1. Il y a une tempête, il y a du **vent**.
2. Je ne vois pas la route devant moi, il y a du **brouillard**.
3. Il fait chaud et il n'y a pas d'air, il fait **lourd**.
4. Les températures sont en-dessous de zéro, il **gèle**.
5. Tout est blanc dehors, il **neige**.
6. Aujourd'hui, il fait **chaud**.
7. Ce matin, il faisait **19** degrés.
8. Ce soir, il va faire **27** degrés.
9. J'adore quand il fait **froid**.
10. Je déteste quand il fait **lourd**.

CHAPTER 31

1. Il est chaud quand on est malade : le **front**
2. Ils ont la même couleur que nos cheveux : les **sourcils**
3. On respire par la bouche ou par le **nez**.
4. On peut y mettre du mascara : les **cils**
5. On voit avec les **yeux**.
6. On entend avec les **oreilles**.
7. Elle pousse sur la partie basse du visage : la **barbe**
8. On montre ses **dents** quand on sourit.
9. La **mâchoire** bouge quand on parle.
10. Le nez a deux **narines**.

CHAPTER 32

Dans mon frigo, il y a
In my fridge, there is

Du broccoli

Du chou-fleur

Des oranges

Des fraises

Un citron

Des pêches

Du beurre

Du lait d'amande

Des yaourts

Des olives

Du ketchup

De la moutarde

De la sauce piquante

Du fromage frais

Du fromage râpé

De la viande

Des œufs

De l'eau pétillante

Du vin blanc

De la bière

CHAPTER 33

1. (un) BRACELET
2. (une) ASSURANCE
3. (un) TOURISTE
4. (une) BOUTEILLE
5. (le) COMMENCEMENT
6. (un) MOUVEMENT
7. (une) RECETTE
8. (un) TABOURET
9. (une) COMPÉTITION
10. (le) VOCABULAIRE
11. (une) RANDONNÉE
12. (un) PASSEPORT
13. (une) TRADUCTION
14. (un) ÉTRANGER
15. PÉTILLANT

CHAPTER 34

Quand j'arrive au travail, je commence par **allumer** mon **ordinateur**. Je tape mon **mot de passe**. Quand mon ordinateur est allumé, j'ouvre ma **boîte de réception** pour lire mes **emails**. J'ai deux **comptes** différents, un pour mes emails privés et un pour mes emails professionnels. Après ça, je vérifie que mon **site internet** fonctionne. Je **clique** sur quelques **pages** pour vérifier les fonctionnalités. Après quelques heures, j'utilise l'**imprimante** pour **imprimer** des contrats. Mes yeux fatiguent vite à force de fixer l'**écran** donc je fais une pause toutes les heures. À la fin de la journée, j'**éteins** mon ordinateur et je branche ma **souris** et mon **clavier** pour les **charger**.

CHAPTER 35

1. **Mon** – ~~Mont~~ – **Mon** rendez-vous vient d'être annulé.
2. ~~ni~~ – **nid** – Les oiseaux construisent un **nid** dans l'arbre.
3. **pain** – ~~pin~~ – J'ai oublié d'acheter du **pain** ce matin.
4. **par** – ~~part~~ – Tu devrais passer **par** ce village pour aller plus vite.
5. ~~pâte~~ – **patte** – Le chien s'est fait mal à la **patte** en jouant.
6. **poêle** – ~~poil~~ – La **poêle** sur le four n'est pas propre.
7. **poids** – ~~pois~~ – Ce n'est pas grave si tu prends un peu de **poids**.
8. ~~poing~~ – **point** – Il faut toujours ajouter un **point** à la fin d'une phrase.
9. ~~près~~ – **prêts** – On sera **prêts** dans une heure.
10. ~~saut~~ – **seau** – Je ne trouve pas le **seau** pour nettoyer.
11. ~~sous~~ – **sou** – Il n'a pas un **sou** dans son portefeuille.
12. **tante** – ~~tente~~ – Ma **tante** vient passer le week-end chez nous.
13. **Vers** – ~~Vert~~ – **Vers** quelle heure est-ce que tu seras là ?
14. **vin** – ~~vingt~~ – Ce **vin** est trop sucré pour moi.
15. ~~vu~~ – **vue** – Ma **vue** n'a pas changé depuis mon dernier examen.

CHAPTER 36

1. C'est le petit de la poule : un **poussin**
2. C'est un animal domestique qui aboie : un **chien**
3. C'est un animal qui miaule et aime les caresses : un **chat**
4. C'est un petit animal à carapace qui marche lentement : une **tortue**
5. C'est un oiseau qui imite les voix humaines : un **perroquet**
6. C'est un animal nocturne qui a de grands yeux : une **chouette**
7. C'est un petit animal qui vit dans les arbres et adore les noisettes : un **écureuil**
8. C'est un animal sauvage qui ressemble à un gros chien et vit en meute : un **loup**
9. C'est un mammifère aquatique qui construit des barrages : un **castor**
10. C'est un animal qui se met en boule pour se protéger : un **hérisson**
11. C'est un animal herbivore qui a des bois sur sa tête : un **cerf**
12. C'est un animal qui peut nager et aime les mares : un **canard**
13. C'est un petit rongeur qui adore les carottes : un **lapin**
14. C'est un reptile qui change de peau et aime le soleil : un **lézard**
15. C'est un animal qui n'aime pas la couleur rouge : un **taureau**

CHAPTER 37

1.	La couture	**Coudre**	**7.**	Le dessin	**Dessiner**
2.	Les langues	**Étudier**	**8.**	Le jardinage	**Jardiner**
3.	La danse	**Danser**	**9.**	Le tricot	**Tricoter**
4.	La peinture	**Peindre**	**10.**	La cuisine	**Cuisiner**
5.	Le camping	**Camper**	**11.**	La lecture	**Lire**
6.	Le chant	**Chanter**			

Pendant mon temps libre, j'aime

tricoter.
jardiner.
faire un puzzle.
lire.
regarder la télévision.

CHAPTER 38

1.	J'assiste à un concert.	Une fois par an
2.	J'écoute de la musique.	Une fois par jour
3.	J'écris à / Je parle avec mes amis et à ma famille.	Plusieurs fois par jour
4.	J'organise un barbecue.	Une fois par an
5.	Je bois du café.	Plusieurs fois par jour
6.	Je fais du camping.	Jamais
7.	Je fais du shopping.	Plusieurs fois par mois
8.	Je fais du sport.	Une fois par jour
9.	Je fais la lessive.	Plusieurs fois par semaine
10.	Je fais les courses.	Plusieurs fois par semaine
11.	Je fais mon lit.	Une fois par jour
12.	Je fais un road trip.	Une fois par an
13.	Je fais une randonnée.	Plusieurs fois par an
14.	Je jardine.	Plusieurs fois par semaine
15.	Je lis / Je regarde les nouvelles.	Plusieurs fois par semaine
16.	Je lis un livre.	Une fois par jour
17.	Je me brosse les dents.	Plusieurs fois par jour
18.	Je nettoie la maison.	Plusieurs fois par semaine
19.	Je participe à un cours de cuisine.	Plusieurs fois par an

20. Je prends le bus.	Plusieurs fois par an
21. Je prends une douche.	Une fois par jour
22. Je prépare le petit déjeuner.	Une fois par jour
23. Je regarde la télévision.	Une fois par jour
24. Je rends visite à ma famille.	Une fois par an
25. Je sors les poubelles.	Jamais
26. Je vais à la plage.	Une fois par an
27. Je vais au restaurant.	Une fois par mois
28. Je vais au travail.	Plusieurs fois par semaine
29. Je vais en vacances.	Une fois par an
30. Je visite un musée.	Une fois par an

CHAPTER 39

CHAPTER 40

1. **V** – Le Louvre est un musée situé à Paris.
2. **F** – Les kangourous vivent en Amérique du Nord. (en Australie)
3. **V** – L'Amazonie est la plus grande forêt tropicale du monde.
4. **F** – La Joconde a été peinte par Van Gogh. (Léonard de Vinci)
5. **V** – Les koalas mangent principalement des feuilles d'eucalyptus.
6. **F** – Le Mexique se trouve en Europe. (en Amérique du Nord)
7. **V** – La Tour de Pise est célèbre pour son inclinaison.
8. **V** – Le plus petit pays du monde est le Vatican.
9. **V** – Les zèbres ont des rayures noires et blanches.
10. **F** – Le français est la langue officielle de l'Allemagne. (l'allemand)
11. **V** – La Statue de la Liberté a été offerte par la France.
12. **F** – La population mondiale dépasse les 10 milliards. (8 milliards)
13. **V** – Les arbres produisent de l'oxygène.
14. **V** – Le chocolat est fabriqué à partir de fèves de cacao.
15. **V** – Le premier homme à marcher sur la lune était Neil Armstrong.
16. **V** – Le cinéma a été inventé par les frères Lumière.
17. **V** – Les échecs sont un jeu de société.
18. **V** – Les diamants peuvent être fabriqués en laboratoire.
19. **F** – La Saint-Valentin est en septembre. (en février)
20. **F** – Pour obtenir la couleur rose, on mélange du rouge et du jaune. (du blanc)

CHAPTER 41

1. J'ai **coincé** la tirette de mon manteau.
   Infinitif : Coincer   Contraire : Décoincer
2. Il **s'est abonné** à plusieurs magazines.
   Infinitif : S'abonner   Contraire : Se désabonner
3. Je **plie** les vêtements avant de les ranger.
   Infinitif : Plier   Contraire : Déplier
4. Elles **se maquillent** tous les jours.
   Infinitif : Se maquiller   Contraire : Se démaquiller
5. Les voyageurs sont en train d'**embarquer**.
   Infinitif : Embarquer   Contraire : Désembarquer
6. N'oublie pas de **boutonner** ta chemise.
   Infinitif : Boutonner   Contraire : Déboutonner

7. Il **gonfle** le ballon de plage pour ses enfants.

Infinitif : Gonfler   Contraire : Dégonfler

8. C'est important de **s'hydrater** quand il fait chaud.

Infinitif : S'hydrater   Contraire : Se déshydrater

9. L'informaticien **installe** le nouveau serveur.

Infinitif : Installer   Contraire : Désinstaller

10. Il me **conseille** d'économiser plus pour acheter une maison.

Infinitif : Conseiller   Contraire : Déconseiller

11. J'**ai approuvé** le budget du nouveau projet.

Infinitif : Approuver   Contraire : Désapprouver

12. On doit **charger** la voiture avant de partir.

Infinitif : Charger   Contraire : Décharger

13. Est-ce que tu **as verrouillé** la porte ?

Infinitif : Verrouiller   Contraire : Déverrouiller

14. Les enfants **obéissent** à leurs parents.

Infinitif : Obéir   Contraire : Désobéir

15. Mon père **monte** la nouvelle bibliothèque dans le garage.

Infinitif : Monter   Contraire : Démonter

CHAPTER 42

Mon mari et moi, on **part en vacances** demain matin. On **va** en Italie. Notre **avion** est à 9 heures du matin. On **a réservé** une semaine dans un **hôtel** près de la plage et on **a loué** une voiture. Je dois encore **faire ma valise** ce soir. J'ai déjà préparé tous mes habits d'été. Le plus important est mon **maillot de bain** car j'adore me baigner, un **livre** pour lire au soleil, et un **chapeau** pour protéger ma tête du soleil. Quand on sera à l'hôtel, on demandera s'ils connaissent un **guide** pour **visiter** la vieille ville. On essaye toujours de faire une ou deux **visites** durant nos **voyages**. Le reste du temps, on le passe à se reposer au bord de la **piscine**.

CHAPTER 43

1. **travail** – ~~travaille~~ – Je commence toujours le **travail** à 9 heures.
2. **bonbon** – ~~bombon~~ – Est-ce que tu veux un **bonbon** ?
3. **environnement** – ~~environnement~~ – C'est important de prendre soin de l'**environnement**.
4. **dîner** – ~~dinner~~ – Le **dîner** est servi.
5. ~~attrapper~~ – **attraper** – Tu vas **attraper** froid si tu ne te couvres pas.
6. ~~appellé~~ – **appelé** – On a **appelé** le voisin mais il n'a pas répondu.

7. feuilles – ~~fueilles~~ – J'ai besoin de plus de **feuilles** de papier.

8. addition – ~~addission~~ – Est-ce que je peux avoir l'**addition** ?

9. ~~siences~~ – sciences – J'aime les **sciences** mais je ne veux pas travailler dans ce domaine.

10. ~~toillettes~~ – toilettes – Les **toilettes** sont hors service.

11. ascenseur – ~~ascenceur~~ – L'**ascenseur** peut accueillir 10 personnes en même temps.

12. ambulance – ~~anbulance~~ – L'**ambulance** est arrivée en moins de trente minutes.

13. ~~envelloppe~~ – enveloppe – Il y a une **enveloppe** dans la boîte aux lettres.

14. automne – ~~autome~~ – L'**automne** a déjà commencé.

15. ~~deuzième~~ – deuxième – C'est la **deuxième** fois qu'on te le demande.

CHAPTER 44

1. Il y a 60 **secondes** dans une minute.

2. Il y a 24 **heures** dans une journée.

3. Il y a 7 **jours** dans une semaine.

4. Un **mois** compte 4 ou 5 semaines.

5. Il y a 10 **ans** dans une décennie.

6. Il y a 7 jours, c'était **la semaine dernière**.

7. **Avant-hier**, c'était le 29 novembre.

8. **Hier**, c'était le 30 novembre.

9. **Demain**, ça sera le 2 décembre.

10. **Après-demain**, ça sera le 3 décembre.

11. Dans 7 jours, ça sera **la semaine prochaine**.

CHAPTER 45

1. Je vais chez des amis pour regarder un **match** de football.

2. Son livre est devenu un **best-seller** en moins de deux semaines.

3. On va souvent au casino mais on n'a jamais gagné le **jackpot**.

4. J'adore manger du **bacon** et des œufs pour le petit déjeuner.

5. Beaucoup de voyageurs prennent des **selfies** devant la tour Eiffel.

6. Va commander à l'intérieur car il y a trop de monde au **drive-in**.

7. Le **show** devait commencer à 19 heures mais il a commencé à 20 heures.

8. Je vais prendre un **sandwich** au jambon et au fromage, s'il vous plaît.

9. Le **meeting** s'est bien déroulé mais il était plus long que prévu.

10. Il y a un grand **parking** près de la gare.

11. Est-ce que tu as assez de viandes pour le **barbecue** ?

12. Mon compte Instagram a atteint 1000 **followers** en quelques mois.

13. L'**airbag** de la voiture s'est déclenché pendant l'accident.

14. Ta fête d'anniversaire était vraiment **fun**.

15. Qu'est-ce que vous prévoyez de faire ce **week-end** ?

CHAPTER 46

1. Chaque soir, je lis un **chapitre** d'un livre avant de dormir.

2. On ne reçoit plus beaucoup de **lettres** de nos jours.

3. Avant de prendre un médicament, c'est bien de lire la **notice**.

4. Je ne trouve pas la **recette** de crêpes que j'utilise toujours.

5. Mon père lit le **journal** tous les matins en buvant son café.

6. Je ne connais pas ce mot. Je vais regarder sa définition au **dictionnaire**.

7. On achète toujours des **magazines** avant de prendre l'avion.

8. Elle oublie toujours ses **manuels scolaires** à l'école.

9. Les acteurs apprennent le **script** par cœur avant de filmer.

10. Je ne trouve pas de **guide de voyage** sur comment voyager seule.

CHAPTER 47

1. Il travaille dans une banque, il est **banquier**.

2. Elle livre le courrier, elle est **factrice**.

3. Il scanne les articles à la caisse du magasin, il est **caissier**.

4. Elle coupe les cheveux, elle est **coiffeuse**.

5. Il soigne les dents, il est **dentiste**.

6. Elle représente ses clients au tribunal, elle est **avocate**.

7. Il s'occupe des patients à l'hôpital, il est **infirmier**.

8. Elle fait partie des forces de l'ordre, elle est **policière**.

9. Il dessine les plans de maisons, il est **architecte**.

10. Elle sert les clients au restaurant, elle est **serveuse**.

11. Il prépare du pain tous les matins, il est **boulanger**.

12. Elle joue de la guitare dans un groupe, elle est **musicienne**.

13. Il va à l'école tous les jours mais il n'est pas professeur, il est **étudiant**.

14. Elle joue dans des films et des séries télévisées, elle est **actrice**.

15. Elle aide les clients au magasin de vêtements, elle est **vendeuse**.

CHAPTER 48

1. Pour aller en vacances, il faut souvent **prendre l'avion**.
2. Les équipes de secours utilisent **un hélicoptère** pour se rendre en montagne.
3. Les enfants **prennent le bus** tous les jours pour aller à l'école.
4. Il y a **un ferry** qui relie ces deux îles.
5. On a acheté **un camping-car** pour visiter les États-Unis.
6. En Europe, on peut **prendre le train** à grande vitesse entre certains pays.
7. Ma fille se déplace toujours **en trottinette**.
8. À New York, **les taxis** sont jaunes.
9. En Italie, beaucoup de touristes louent **des scooters**.
10. Mes grands-parents ont acheté **deux vélos électriques**.
11. La capitaine **navigue le bateau** à travers l'océan.
12. Je **fais du covoiturage** avec mes collègues pour aller au travail.
13. On **a réservé un taxi** pour aller à l'aéroport.
14. **Monter dans le train** peut être difficile pour certains.
15. Je vais à la boulangerie **à pied** car elle est proche de chez moi.

CHAPTER 49

1. ~~débordé~~ – **désolé** – Je suis **désolé** de ne pas avoir pu venir à ton mariage.
2. **énervé** – ~~fière~~ – Il était **énervé** mais je ne sais pas pourquoi.
3. **inquiets** – ~~honteux~~ – Mes parents sont **inquiets** car ils n'ont pas de nouvelles de mon frère.
4. **heureux** – ~~terrorisés~~ – On est **heureux** d'avoir fini nos études.
5. **fatiguée** – ~~contente~~ – Tu es **fatiguée** car tu n'as pas assez dormi.
6. ~~pessimiste~~ – **gêné** – Elle est toujours **gêné** de parler en public.
7. ~~nerveux~~ – **fier** – Tu peux être **fier** de toi.
8. ~~impatient~~ – **malheureux** – Il est **malheureux** depuis son divorce.
9. ~~fatigués~~ – **amoureux** – Ils sont follement **amoureux** l'un de l'autre.
10. **nerveux** – ~~perdu~~ – Le patient est **nerveux** avant son examen.
11. **épanouie** – ~~crevée~~ – C'est bien de te voir **épanouie**.
12. ~~vidés~~ – **déçus** – Ils étaient **déçus** que tu ne sois pas venu.
13. ~~joyeux~~ – **furieux** – Son père était **furieux** quand il a eu son accident.
14. **impatient** – ~~triste~~ – Le train va bientôt arriver. Ne sois pas aussi **impatient**.
15. **découragés** – ~~fatigués~~ – Les élèves sont **découragés** après avoir eu de mauvaises notes.

CHAPTER 50

1. C'est le fils de ma sœur, c'est mon **neveu**.
2. Je suis la marraine du fils de mes amis, c'est mon **filleul**.
3. C'est la mère de mon père, c'est ma **grand-mère**.
4. C'est le mari de ma mère mais ce n'est pas mon père, c'est mon **beau-père**.
5. C'est la fille de ma grand-mère mais ce n'est pas ma mère, c'est ma **tante**.
6. C'est la personne que j'ai épousée, c'est mon **mari**.
7. Je suis le plus âgé de mes frères et sœurs, je suis l'**aîné**.
8. Mes frères sont nés le même jour, ce sont des **jumeaux**.
9. C'est la fille de la sœur de mon mari, c'est ma **nièce**.
10. Je suis la filleule de la meilleure amie de ma mère, c'est ma **marraine**.
11. C'est le fils de mon fils, c'est mon **petit-fils**.
12. Je suis la plus jeune de mes frères et sœurs, je suis la **cadette**.
13. C'est la fille de ma tante, c'est ma **cousine**.
14. Ce sont toutes les personnes de ma famille, ce sont mes **proches**.
15. C'est le fils de ma mère et de mon beau-père, c'est mon **demi-frère**.

FRENCH-ENGLISH GLOSSARY

A

Une abeille nf | A bee

Un abonné - Une abonnée n | A subscriber

Un abonnement nm | A subscription

Aboyer v | To bark

Un abricot nm | An apricot

Un abricotier nm | An apricot tree

Un accident nm | An accident

Acheter v | To buy

Un acteur - Une actrice n | An actor

Activer v | To activate

Accueillir v | To welcome

Une addition nf | A bill

Une adresse email nf | An email address

Là adv | Here - There

Un aéroport nm | An airport

Affectueux - Affectueuse adj | Affectionate

Une affiche nf | A poster

Un - Une agent de voyage n | A travel agent

Un agneau nm | A lamb

Un agriculteur - Une agricultrice n | A farmer

Aimer v | To like - To love

L'aîné nm | The oldest

L'aînée nf | The oldest

Un airbag nm

Ajouter v | To add

L'Allemagne nf | Germany

Aller v | To go

Aller à pied | To go by foot

Aller à quelqu'un | To suit someone

Aller au cinéma | To go to the theater

Aller en métro | To go by subway

Aller en train | To go by train

Aller en voiture | To go by car

Aller bien v | To suit

Allez (filler word) | Come on - Let's go

Allumer v | To turn on

Une amande nf | An almond

L'Amazonie nf | The Amazon

Une ambulance nf | An ambulance

L'Amérique du Nord nf | North America

Un ami - Une amie n | A friend

Une amende nf | A fine

L'amour nm | Love

Un an nm | A year

Ancien - Ancienne adj | Old

Une ancre nf | An anchor

Un âne nm | A donkey

Un animal nm | An animal

Une année nf | A year

L'année dernière | Last year

L'année prochaine | Next year

Une année scolaire nf | A school year

Un anniversaire nm | A birthday

L'annulaire nm | Ring finger

Antipathique adj | Unfriendly

Un appareil photo nm | A camera

Apparemment adv | Apparently

Appeler v | To call

Des applaudissements nm | Applause

Une application - Une appli nf |
An application - An app

Apprendre v | To learn

Apprivoisé - Apprivoisée adj | Tamed

Approuver v | To approve

Après-demain adv | The day after tomorrow

Un après-midi nm | An afternoon

L'après-shampoing nm | Conditioner

Août nm | August

Un arbre nm | A tree

Un arc-en-ciel nm | A rainbow

Un - Une architecte n | An architect

Armer v | To arm

Une armoire nf | A wardrobe

Arracher les mauvaises herbes |
To pull up weeds

L'arrivée nf | Arrival

Arroser v | To water

Arroser les plantes | To water the plant

La art | *The*

L'art dramatique nm | Acting

Un article nm | *An article*

Artificiel - Artificielle adj | *Artificial*

ASAP (As soon as possible)

Un ascenseur nm | *An elevator*

Assaisonner v | *To season*

Une assiette nf | *A plate*

Un assistant - Une assistante n | *An assistant*

Assister v | *To attend*

Un - Une astronaute n | *An astronaut*

Un atelier nm | *A workshop*

Attendre le bus | *To wait for the bus*

Attraper froid | *To catch a cold*

L'aube nf | *Dawn*

Aujourd'hui adv | *Today*

L'auriculaire nm | *Litlle finger*

L'automne nm | *Autumn - Fall*

L'avant-bras nm | *Forearm*

Avant-hier adv | *The day before yesterday*

Un avocat nm | *An avocado*

Un avocatier nm | *An avocado tree*

Avoir ... ans | *To be ... years old*

Avoir besoin de | *To need*

Avoir chaud | *To be hot*

Avoir de la chance | *To be lucky*

Avoir envie de | *To want*

Avoir faim | *To be hungry*

Avoir froid | *To be cold*

Avoir mal à + body part | *To have an ache*

Avoir mal à la gorge | *To have a sore throat*

Avoir mal à la tête | *To have a headache*

Avoir mal au dos | *To have back pain*

Avoir mal au ventre | *To have a stomach ache*

Avoir mal aux dents | *To have a toothache*

Avoir mauvaise conscience | *To have a guilty conscience*

Avoir peur | *To be afraid*

Avoir soif | *To be thirsty*

Avoir sommeil | *To be sleepy*

Un avion nm | *A plane*

Un avocat - Une avocate n | *A lawyer*

Avril nm | *April*

B

Un - Une baby-sitter n

Un bagage nm | *A baggage*

Un bagage à main nm | *A carry-on*

Du bain de bouche nm | *Mouthwash*

Une baignoire nf | *A bathtub*

Une balance nf | *A scale*

Une balançoire nf | *A swing*

Un balayage nm | *A balayage*

Une balle nf | *A ball*

Un ballon nm | *A balloon*

Une banane nf | *A banana*

Un bananier nm | *A banana tree*

Une bande dessinée nf | *A comic*

Un banquier - Une banquière n | *A banker*

Un bar nm

La barbe nf | *Beard*

Un barbecue nm | *A barbecue*

Bas - Basse | *Low*

Le basketball nm

Des baskets nf | *Sneakers*

Un bateau nm | *A boat*

Battre v | *To whisk*

Bavard - Bavarde adj | *Talkative*

Beau - Belle adj | *Beautiful*

Un beau-fils nm | *A son-in-law - A stepson*

Un beau-frère nm | *A brother-in-law - A stepbrother*

Un beau-père nm | *A father-in-law - A stepfather*

Les beaux-parents nm | *The parents-in-law - Stepparents*

Une belle-fille nf | *A daughter-in-law - A stepdaughter*

Une belle-mère nf | *A mother-in-law - A stepmother*

Une belle-sœur nf | *A sister-in-law - A stepsister*

Beige adj | *Beige*

Un best-seller nm

Du beurre nm | *Butter*

Une bibliothèque nf | *A library*
Une bibliothèque universitaire nf |
A university library
Une bicyclette nf | *A bike*
De la bière nf | *Beer*
Les bijoux nm | *Jewelry making*
Blanc - Blanche adj | *White*
Bleu - Bleue adj | *Blue*
Un blog nm | *A blog*
Blond - Blonde adj | *Blonde*
Bloquer v | *To block*
Boire v | *To drink*
Une boîte aux lettres nf | *A mailbox*
Une boîte de nf | *A box of - A can of*
Une boîte de réception nf | *An inbox*
Un bol nm | *A bowl*
Un bol - Une gamelle n | *A bowl*
Bon - Bonne adj | *Good*
Bon marché adj | *Cheap*
Un bonbon nm | *A candy*
Une bonne recette | *A good recipe*
Un bon restaurant | *A good restaurant*
Un bonbon nm | *A candy*
Des bottes nf | *Boots*
La bouche nf | *Mouth*
Un boucher - Une bouchère n | *A butcher*
Une boucherie nf | *A butcher*
La boue nf | *Mud*
Une bougie nf | *A candle*
Bouillir v | *To boil*
Un boulanger - Une boulangère n | *A baker*
Une boulangerie nf | *A bakery*
Une boule de poils nf | *A hairball*
Une bouilloire nf | *A kettle*
Une bourse d'études nf | *A scholarship*
Un bout nm | *A piece*
Une bouteille de nf | *A bottle of*
Boutonner v | *To button*
Le bowling nm
Brancher v | *To plug*
Le bras nm | *Arm*
Du brocoli nm | *Broccoli*
Une brosse nf | *A brush*

Une brosse à dents nf | *A toothbrush*
Une brosse à dents électrique nf |
An electric toothbrush
Un buisson nm | *A bush*
Brancher v | *To plug*
Une brochure nf | *A brochure*
Brun - Brune - Marron adj | *Brown*
Un brushing nm | *A brushing*
Une buanderie nf | *A laundry room*
Un building nm
Un bureau nm | *An office*
Un bureau de poste nm | *A post office*
Le bus nm | *The bus*
Le business nm

C

Ça pr | *That*
Un cadeau nm | *A gift*
Le cadet nm | *The youngest*
La cadette nf | *The youngest*
Un café nm | *A coffee*
Une cafetière nf | *A coffee machine*
Un cahier nm | *A notebook*
Un caissier - Une caissière n | *A cashier*
La calligraphie nf | *Calligraphy*
Un camion nm | *A truck*
Un camp nm | *A camp*
Du camping nm | *Camping*
Un camping-car nm | *A camper van*
Un canapé nm | *A couch*
Un canard nm | *A duck*
Une canette de nf | *A can of*
La capitale nf | *The capital*
Un car nm | *A bus*
Car conj | *For - Because*
Une caravane nf | *A caravan*
Caresser v | *To pet*
Des carottes nf | *Carrots*
Un carré nm | *A square*
Une carte nf | *A card*
Une carte nf | *A map*
Une carte de crédit nf | *A credit card*

Une casserole nf | *A pot*
Un cassis nm | *A blackcurrant*
Un cassissier nm | *A blackcurrant bush*
Un casting nm
Un castor nm | *A beaver*
Une cave nf | *A cellar*
Ce pr | *This*
Célèbre adj | *Famous*
Un cerf nm | *A deer*
Une cerise nf | *A cherry*
Le cinéma nm | Cinema
Des ciseaux nm | *Scissors*
Du céleri nm | *Celery*
Cent n | *One hundred*
Un centre commercial nm | *A shopping center*
Un cercle nm | *A circle*
Un cerisier nm | *A cherry tree*
Le cerveau nm | *Brain*
Une chaîne nf | *A channel*
Une chaise nf | *A chair*
Une chaise d'extérieur nf | *An outdoor chair*
Une chaise longue nf | *A lounge chair*
Un challenge nm
Une chambre nf | *A bedroom*
Une chambre d'amis nf | *A guest room*
Un champ de lavande nm | *A lavender field*
Des champignons nm | *Mushrooms*
Un chanteur - Une chanteuse n | *A singer*
De la charcuterie nf | *Deli meat*
Charger v | *To load*
Le charme nf | *Charm*
Le chant nm | *Singing*
Chanter v | *To sing*
Un chapeau nm | *A hat*
Chargé - Chargée adj | *Busy*
Charger v | *To charge*
Un chat nm | *A cat*
Une chatte nf | *A female cat*
Un chaton nm | *A kitten*
Chaud - Chaude adj | *Hot*
Chauffer v | *To heat*
Un chauffeur - Une chauffeuse n | *A driver*
Des chaussettes nf | *Socks*

Des chaussures nf | *Shoes*
Des chaussures à talons nf | *High-heel shoes*
Des chaussures plates nf | *Flat-heel shoes*
Une chauve-souris nf | *A bat*
Une chemise nf | *A shirt*
Cher - Chère adj | *Expensive*
Un cheval nm | *A horse*
Les cheveux nm | *Hair*
Les cheveux bouclés adj | *Curly hair*
Les cheveux courts adj | *Short hair*
Les cheveux longs adj | *Long hair*
Les cheveux ondulés adj | *Wavy hair*
Les cheveux raides - lisses adj | *Straight hair*
La cheville nf | *Ankle*
Une chèvre nf | *A goat*
Un chien nm | *A dog*
Un chien d'assistance nm | *A service dog*
Un chien guide nm | *A guide dog*
Une chienne nf | *A female dog*
Un chignon nm | *A bun*
Un chirurgien - Une chirurgienne n |
A surgeon
Un chiot nm | *A puppy*
Le chocolat nm | *Chocolate*
Du chou-fleur nm | *Cauliflower*
Une chouette nf | *An owl*
Les cils nm | *Eyelashes*
Le cinéma nm | *Cinema*
Le cinéma nm | *The theater*
Une circonstance nf | *A circumstance*
Des ciseaux nm | *Scissors*
Un citron nm | *A lemon*
Un citronnier nm | *A lemon tree*
Un clavier nm | *A keyboard*
Cliquer v | *To click*
Une clôture nf | *A fence*
Un clown nm | *A clown*
Un cocotier nm | *A coconut tree*
Un cochon nm | *A pig*
Un cochon d'inde nm | *A guinea pig*
Un coach nm
Un cocktail nm
Un coiffeur - Une coiffeuse n | *A hairdresser*

Coincer v | *To stick*
La colère nf | *Anger*
Une collection nf | *A collection*
Coller v | *To paste*
Un collier nm | *A collar*
Une coloration nf | *A colour*
Un comédien - Une comédienne n |
A comedian
Commander en ligne v | *To order online*
Commencer v | *To start*
Un commentaire nm | *A comment*
Comprendre v | *To learn*
La compréhension nf | *Comprehension*
Un - Une comptable n | *An accountant*
Comptant adj | *Cash*
Un compte nm | *An account*
Un concert nm | *A concert*
Du concombre nm | *Cucumber*
Conduire v | *To drive*
Un cône nm | *A cone*
Une conférence nf | *A lecture*
Un congélateur nm | *A freezer*
Connecter v | *To connect*
Conseiller v | *To advise*
Un conseiller - Une conseillère n |
A consultant
Content adj | *Happy*
Le contenu nm | *The content*
Copier v | *To copy*
Un coq nm | *A rooster*
Le cou nm | *Neck*
Le coude nm | *Elbow*
Couler v | *To sink*
Une couleur nf | *A colour*
Un couloir nm | *A hallway*
Le coup nm | *Shot*
Une coupe nf | *A cut*
Une coupe de cheveux nf | *A haircut*
Couper v | *To cut*
Couper en dés v | *To dice*
Couper en lamelles v | *To slice*
Courageux - Courageuse | *Brave*
Couramment adv | *Fluently*

De la courgette nm | *Zucchini*
Un cours nm | *A course*
Un cours de cuisine nm | *A cooking class*
Les courses nf | *Grocery shopping*
Court - Courte Adj | *Short*
Un cousin nm | *A cousin*
Une cousine nf | *A cousin*
Le coût nm | *Cost*
Un couteau nm | *A knife*
Un couteau à pain nm | *A bread knife*
La couture nf | *Sewing*
Les couverts nm | *Cutlery - Silverware*
Couvrir v | *To cover*
Un cowboy nm
Un coyote nm | *A coyote*
Le cœur nm | *Heart*
Un crash nm
De la crème nf | *Cream*
De la crème solaire nf | *Sunscreen*
Le crépuscule nm | *Dusk*
Creuser v | *To dig*
Le crochet nm | *Crocheting*
Une croisière nf | *A cruise*
Un croissant nm | *A crescent*
Des croquettes nf | *Dry food*
Un cube nm | *A cube*
Cueillir v | *To pick*
Une cuillère nf | *A spoon*
Une cuillère à café nf | *A teaspoon*
Une cuillère à soupe nf | *A tablespoon*
Une cuillère en bois nf | *A woodspoon*
Cuire à la vapeur v | *To steam*
Cuire au four v | *To bake*
La cuisine nf | *Cooking*
La cuisine nf | *The kitchen*
Cuisiner v | *To cook*
Un cuisinier - Une cuisinière n | *A cook*
Une cuisinière nf | *A stove*
Une cuisinière à gaz nf | *A gas stove*
La cuisse nf | *Thigh*
Cultiver v | *To cultivate*
Le cygne nm | *Swan*
Un cylindre nm | *A cylinder*

D

Dans prep | In
Une danse nf | A dance
La danse nf | Dancing
Un danseur - Une danseuse n | A dancer
Un dauphin nm | A dolphin
Un débarras nm | A storage room
Déboutonner v | To unbutton
Débrancher v | To unplug
Décembre nm | December
Une décennie nf | A decade
Décharger v | To unload
Décoincer v | To unstick
Déconnecter v | To disconnect
Déconseiller v | To advise against
Découvrir v | To uncover
Défaire v | To undo
Défroisser v | To smooth out
Dégonfler v | To deflate
Les décorations nf | Decorations
Un degré nm | A degree
Déguster v | To enjoy
Une demande d'ami nf | A friend request
Demain adv | Tomorrow
Demander v | To ask - To fill
Un demi-frère nm | A half-brother
Une demi-heure nf | Half an hour
Une demi-lune nf | A half-moon
Une demi-sœur nf | A half-sister
Démonter v | To disassemble
Une dent nf | A tooth
Un - Une dentiste n | A dentist
Les dents nf | The teeth
Du fil dentaire nm | Floss
Du dentifrice nm | Toothpaste
Le déodorant nm | Deodorant
Le départ nm | Departure
Dépasser v | To exceed
Déplier v | To unfold
Déranger v | To mess up
Dernier - Dernière adj | Last

Désactiver v | To deactivate
Désapprouver v | To disapprove
Désarmer v | To disarm
Descendre du métro | To get off the subway
Désembarquer v | To disembark
Déséquilibrer v | To unbalance
Déshumidifier v | To dehumidify
Un design nm
Désinfecter v | To disinfect
Désinstaller v | To uninstall
Désobéir v | To disobey
Désorganisé - Désorganisée | Disorganized
Le dessin nm | Drawing
Une destination nf | A destination
Deuxième | Second
Déverrouiller v | To unlock
Un devoir nm | Homework
Un diamant nm | A diamond
Un dictionnaire nm | A dictionary
Difficile adj | Difficult
Dimanche nm | Sunday
Le dimanche nm | Sunday
Une dinde nf | A turkey
Le dîner nm | Dinner
Un diplôme nm | A diploma
Un discount nm
Discuter v | To talk
Un disque dur nm | A hard drive
Une dissertation nf | An essay
Distinct - Distincte adj | Distinct
Un directeur - Une directrice n | A director
Un divorce nm | A divorce
La douane nf | Customs
Un docteur - Une docteure n | A doctor
Un documentaire nm | A documentary
Le doigt nm | Finger
Le doigt de pied - L'orteil nm | Toe
Un domaine nm | A field
Un domicile nm | From home
Le dos nm | Back
Un dossier nm | A folder
Une douche nf | A shower
Dresser v | To train

Un dressing nm | *A walk-in closet*
Le drive-in nm
Dur - Dure adj | *Hard*

E

L'eau nf | *Water*
De l'eau pétillante nf | *Sparkling water*
Un e-book nm | *An e-book*
Échanger v | *To exchange*
Les échecs nm | *Chess*
Une école nf | *A school*
Écouter v | *To listen*
Un écran nm | *A screen*
Écraser v | *To crush*
Écrire v | *To write*
Un écureuil nm | *A squirrel*
Égoutter v | *To drain*
Un égouttoir nm | *A dish rack*
Un élan nm | *A moose*
Un électricien - Une électricienne n |
An electrician
Un éléphant nm | *An elephant*
Un - Une élève n | *A student*
Un éleveur nm | *A breeder*
Un email nm | *An email*
Un emballage nm | *Wrap*
Embarquer v | *To embark*
Un emoji nm | *An emoji*
En adv | *Some*
En prep | *To - In*
En ligne adj | *Online*
En panne adj | *Broken*
De l'encre nf | *Ink*
Une encyclopédie nf | *An encyclopedia*
Les enfants nm | *The children*
Enfourner v | *To put in the oven*
Enlever v | *To take off*
Ennuyant - Ennuyante adj | *Boring*
Une enveloppe nf | *An envelope*
L'environnement nm | *The environment*
L'épaule nf | *Shoulder*
Une épicerie nf | *A grocery store*

Des épinards nm | *Spinach*
Éplucher v | *To peel*
Un éplucheur nm | *A peeler*
Éprouvant - Éprouvante adj | *Challenging*
Un érable nm | *A maple tree*
Les escaliers nm | *The stairs*
Essayer v | *To try on*
Une essoreuse à salade nf | *A salad spinner*
L'est nm | *East*
L'estomac nm | *Stomach*
Une étagère nf | *A shelf*
L'été nm | *Summer*
Éteindre v | *To turn off*
Une étoile nf | *A star*
Être + nationality | *To be + nationality*
Être à l'heure | *To be on time*
Être à quelqu'un | *To belong to somebody*
Être abonné(e) v | *To be subscribed*
Être amoureux - amoureuse | *To be in love*
Être angoissé - angoissée | *To be anguished*
Être anxieux - anxieuse | *To be anxious*
Être au courant | *To be informed*
Être connu(e) v | *To be known*
Être content - contente | *To be happy*
Être crevé - crevée | *To be tired*
Être d'accord | *To agree*
Être de | *To be from*
Être de bonne humeur |
To be in a good mood
Être de mauvaise humeur |
To be in a bad mood
Être de retour | *To be back*
Être débordé - débordée |
To be overwhelmed
Être découragé - découragée |
To be discouraged
Être déçu - déçue | *To be disappointed*
Être dégoûté - dégoûtée | *To be disgusted*
Être écœuré - écœurée | *To be disgusted*
Être en colère | *To be angry*
Être énervé - énervée | *To be mad*
Être fâché - fâchée | *To be angry*
Être frustré - frustrée | *To be frustrated*

Être furieux - furieuse | *To be furious*
Être hors de soi | *To be out of oneself*
Être démoralisé - démoralisée |
To be demoralized
Être démotivé - démotivée |
To be demotivated
Être déprimé - déprimée | *To be depressed*
Être désespéré - désespérée |
To be desperate
Être désolé - désolée | *To be sorry*
Être dévasté - dévastée | *To be devastated*
Être effrayé - effrayée | *To be scared*
Être inquiet - inquiète | *To be worried*
Être en avance | *To be early*
Être en bonne santé | *To be healthy*
Être en colère | *To be angry*
Être en retard | *To be late*
Être en train de (+ inf) | *To be in the*
process of (doing)
Être enchanté - enchantée | *To be enchanted*
Être épanoui - épanouie | *To be fulfilled*
Être épuisé - épuisée | *To be exhausted*
Être fatigué - fatiguée | *To be tired*
Être fabriqué - fabriquée | *To be made*
Être fier - fière | *To be proud*
Être fou - folle de | *To be crazy about*
Être passionné - passionnée |
To be passionate
Être gêné - gênée | *To be embarrassed*
Être heureux - heureuse | *To be happy*
Être honteux - honteuse | *To be ashamed*
Être impatient - impatiente | *To be excited*
Être joyeux - joyeuse | *To be happy*
Être malheureux - malheureuse | *To be sad*
Être mécontent - mécontente |
To be dissatisfied
Être nerveux - nerveuse | *To be nervous*
Être paniqué - paniquée | *To be panicked*
Être optimiste | *To be optimistic*
Être perdu - perdue | *To be lost*
Être pessimiste | *To be pessimistic*
Être ravi - ravie | *To be delighted*
Être servi - servie | *To be served*

Être situé - située | *To be located*
Être stressé - stressée | *To be stressed*
Être terrifié - terrifiée | *To be terrified*
Être terrorisé - terrorisée | *To be terrorized*
Être sur le point de (+ inf) | *To be about to (do)*
Être triste | *To be sad*
Être vidé - vidée | *To be drained*
Les études nf | *Studies*
Un étudiant - Une étudiante n | *A student*
Étudier v | *To study*
L'Europe nf | *Europe*
Une évaluation nf | *An assessment*
Un évier nm | *A sink*
Un examen nm | *An exam*
Une exception nf | *An exception*
Une excursion nf | *An excursion*
Un exercice nm | *An exercise*
Une exit nf
Extraverti(e) adj | *Extroverted*

F

Facile adj | *Easy*
Un facteur - Une factrice n |
A postman - A postwoman
Une faculté nf | *A faculty*
Faible adj | *Weak*
La faim nf | *Hunger*
Faire v | *To do*
Faire attention | *To pay attention*
Faire bouillir | *To boil*
Faire cuire | *To cook*
Faire de la calligraphie |
To practice calligraphy
Faire de la danse - Danser | *To dance*
Faire de la menuiserie | *To do woodworking*
Faire de la natation | *To swim*
Faire de la pâtisserie | *To bake*
Faire de la peinture - Peindre | *To paint*
Faire de la philatélie | *To collect stamps*
Faire de la photographie | *To do photography*
Faire de la poterie | *To do pottery*
Faire de la randonnée | *To hike*

THE PERFECT FRENCH WITH DYLANE | FRENCH VOCABULARY WORKBOOK

Faire de la sculpture | *To sculpt*
Faire des bijoux | *To make jewelry*
Faire des fautes | *To make mistakes*
Faire des mots croisés | *To do crosswords*
Faire des progrès | *To make progress*
Faire du camping - Camper | *To camp*
Faire du chant - Chanter | *To sing*
Faire du compost | *To compost*
Faire du covoiturage | *To carpool*
Faire du crochet | *To crochet*
Faire du cyclisme | *To bike*
Faire du dessin - Dessiner | *To draw*
Faire du football | *To play soccer*
Faire du jardinage - Jardiner | *To garden*
Faire du savo n | *To make soap*
Faire du shopping | *To go shopping*
Faire du sport - de l'exercice | *To exercise*
Faire du théâtre | *To play*
Faire du tricot - Tricoter | *To knit*
Faire du vélo | *To bike*
Faire fondre | *To melt*
Faire la cuisine | *To cook*
Faire la lessive | *To do the laundry*
Faire la tête | *To be moody*
Faire la vaisselle | *To do the dishes*
Faire le ménage | *To do the cleaning*
Faire les courses | *To shop*
Faire peur (à) | *To scare*
Faire pousser | *To grow*
Faire revenir | *To brown*
Faire sa valise | *To pack*
Faire sauter | *To saute*
Faire ses devoirs | *To do one's homework*
Faire son lit | *To make one's bed*
Faire un puzzle | *To make a puzzle*
Faire un voyage | *To take a trip*
Faire une promenade | *To take a walk*
Une famille nf | *A family*
Le fard (à paupières) nm | *Make-up*
La fatigue nf | *Tiredness*
Fatigué - Fatiguée adj | *Tired*
Un fauteuil nm | *An armchair*
Une femme nf | *A wife*

Une femme au foyer n | *A housewife*
Fermé - Fermée adj | *Closed*
Une fenêtre nf | *A window*
Un fermier - Une fermière n | *A farmer*
Un ferry nm | *A ferry*
Les fesses nf | *Buttocks*
Une fête nf | *A party*
Fêter v | *To celebrate*
Un feu nm | *A fire pit*
Une feuille d'eucalyptus nf |
An eucalyptus leaf
Une feuille de papier nf | *A piece of paper*
Une fève de cacao nf | *A cocoa bean*
Février nm | *February*
Un fichier nm | *A file*
Fidèle adj | *Faithful*
Une figue nf | *A fig*
Un figuier nm | *A fig tree*
Un fil d'actualité nm | *A wall - A feed*
Une fille nf | *A daughter*
Un filleul nm | *A godson*
Une filleule nf | *A goddaughter*
Un film nm | *A movie*
La fin nf | *End*
Le fitness nm
Un fils nm | *A son*
Un flash-back nm
Une fleur nf | *A flower*
Fleurir v | *To blossom*
Un fleuriste nm | *A flower shop*
Un flyer nm
La foi nf | *Faith*
Le foie nm | *Liver*
Une fois nf | *Once - One time*
Un follower nm
Le football nm
Une forêt tropicale nf | *A tropical rainforest*
Une formation nf | *Training*
Fort - Forte adj | *Strong*
Un fouet nm | *A whisk*
Fouetter v | *To whisk*
Un four nm | *An oven*
Une fourchette nf | *A fork*

La fourrure nf | *Fur*
Une fraise nf | *A strawberry*
Un fraisier nm | *A strawberry plant*
Une framboise nf | *A raspberry*
Un framboisier nm | *A raspberry bush*
Le français nm | *French*
La France nf | *France*
Une frange nf | *Bangs*
Un frère nm | *A brother*
Frire v | *To fry*
Froid - Froide adj | *Cold*
Froisser v | *To crumple*
Du fromage nm | *Cheese*
Du fromage blanc nm | *Cream cheese*
Du fromage râpé nm | *Grated cheese*
Le front nm | *Forehead*
Frustré - Frustrée adj | *Frustrated*
Fun adj

G

Un garage nm | *A garage*
Une gare nf | *A train station*
Gâté - Gâtée adj | *Spoiled*
Un gâteau nm | *A cake*
Le gel douche nm | *Shower gel*
Geler v | *To freeze*
Un gène nm | *A gene*
La gêne nf | *Embarrassment*
Le genou nm | *Knee*
Gentil - Gentille adj | *Kind*
Un gilet nm | *A cardigan*
Gonfler v | *To inflate*
Goûter v | *To taste*
La grammaire nf | *Grammar*
Un gramme nm | *A gram*
Grand - Grande adj | *Tall*
Une grand-mère nf | *A grandmother*
La Grande Muraille de Chine nf | *The Great Wall of China*
Les grands-parents nm | *The grandparents*
Un grand-père nm | *A grandfather*
Un - Une graphiste n | *A graphic designer*

Un gratte-ciel nm | *A skyscraper*
Une grenade nf | *A pomegranate*
Un grenadier nm | *A pomegranate tree*
Un grenier nm | *An attic*
Les griffes nf | *Claws*
Un griffoir nm | *A scratching pole*
Un grille-pain nm | *A toaster*
Gris - Grise adj | *Grey*
Une groseille nf | *A currant*
Un groseillier nm | *A currant bush*
Un groupe nm | *A group*
Un guide nm | *A guide*
Un guide de voyage nm | *A travel guide*
Une guitare nf | *A guitar*

H

Hacher v | *To chop*
Une haie nf | *A hedge*
Un hall d'entrée nm | *An entrance*
Un hamac nm | *A hammock*
Un hamster nm | *A hamster*
La hanche nf | *Hip*
Des haricots verts nm | *Green beans*
Un harnais nm | *A harness*
Un hashtag nm
Haut - Haute adj | *High*
Un haut-parleur nm | *A speaker*
Un hélicoptère nm | *A helicopter*
Un hérisson nm | *A hedgehog*
Une heure nf | *An hour*
Heureux - Heureuse adj | *Happy*
Un hexagone nm | *A hexagon*
Hier adv | *Yesterday*
L'hiver nm | *Winter*
Le hockey nm | *Hockey*
Un holdup nm
Un homme au foyer n | *A househusband*
Un homme d'affaires - Une femme d'affaires n | *A businessman - A businesswoman*
La honte nf | *Shame*
Un hôpital nm | *A hospital*
Le hoquet nm | *Hiccup*

Hors ligne adj | *Offline*
Hors service adj | *Out of order*
Un hôtel nm | *A hotel*
L'hôtel de ville - La mairie n | *City Hall*
Le houx nm | *Holly*
Humide adj | *Wet*
Humidifier v | *To humidify*

I

Il pr | *He - It*
Il - Elle a les cheveux ... | *He - she has ... hair*
Il - elle est ... | *He - she is ...*
Il fait 3 degrés | *It's 3 degrees*
Il fait beau | *It's nice out*
Il fait chaud | *It's hot*
Il fait frais | *It's cool - chilly*
Il fait froid | *It's cold*
Il fait humide | *It's humid*
Il fait lourd | *It's muggy*
Il fait mauvais | *It's bad weather*
Il fait moins 4 | *It's minus 4*
Il fait nuageux | *It's cloudy*
Il fait orageux | *It's stormy*
Il fait soleil | *It's sunny*
Il gèle (geler) | *It's freezing (to freeze)*
Il grêle (grêler) | *It's hailing (to hail)*
Il neige (neiger) | *It's snowing (to snow)*
Il pleut (pleuvoir) | *It's raining (to rain)*
Il y a du brouillard | *It's foggy*
Il y a du soleil | *It's sunny*
Il y a du vent | *It's windy*
Il y a une tempête de neige | *It's a snowstorm*
Un îlot de cuisine nm | *A kitchen island*
Ils pr | *They*
Immédiat - Immédiate adj | *Immediate*
Un immeuble à appartements nm |
An apartment building
Un immeuble de bureaux nm |
An office building
Impatient - Impatiente adj | *Impatient*
Une imprimante nf | *A printer*
Imprimer v | *To print*

Impoli - Impolie adj | *Rude*
Important - Importante adj | *Important*
Une inclinaison nf | *A tilt*
Incorporer v | *To stir in*
L'index nm | *Index*
Infecter v | *To infect*
Infidèle adj | *Unfaithful*
Un infirmier - Une infirmière n | *A nurse*
Un informaticien - Une informaticienne n |
A computer scientist
L'informatique nm | *IT*
Un ingénieur - Une ingénieure n |
An engineer
Installer v | *To install*
Un instituteur - Une institutrice n |
A primary school teacher
Interminable adj | *Endless*
Internet nm | *The Internet*
Un interview nm
L'intestin nm | *Intestine*
Introverti(e) adj | *Introverted*
Inutile adj | *Useless*
Une invitation nf | *An invitation*
Un invité - Une invitée n | *A guest*
L'Italie nf | *Italy*
Un itinéraire nm | *A route*

J

Un jackpot nm
La jambe nf | *Leg*
Janvier nm | *January*
Le Japon nm | *Japan*
Un jardin nm | *A garden*
Le jardinage nm | Gardening
Jardiner v | *To garden*
Jaune adj | *Yellow*
Un jean nm
Un jeu nm | *A game*
Un jeu de société nm | *A board game*
Jeudi nm | *Thursday*
Jeune adj | *Young*
Les jeux vidéo nm | *Video games*

La Joconde nf | *The Mona Lisa*

Un job nm

La joie - Le bonheur | *Happiness*

Une joue nf | *A cheek*

Jouer v | *To play*

Jouer aux échecs | *To play chess*

Jouer aux jeux de société |
To play board games

Jouer aux jeux vidéo | *To play video games*

Jouer de la musique | *To play music*

Un jouet nm | *A toy*

Un jour nm | *A day*

Un journal nm | *A newspaper*

Un - Une journaliste n | *A journalist*

Une journée nf | *A day*

Les jours de la semaine | *Days of the week*

Juillet nm | *July*

Juin nm | *June*

Des jumeaux nm | *Twins*

Des jumelles nf | *Twins*

Une jupe nf | *A skirt*

Du jus d'orange nm | *Orange juice*

K

Un kaki nm | *A persimmon*

Un kaki nm | *A persimmon tree*

Un kangourou nm | *A kangaroo*

Du ketchup nm | *Ketchup*

Un kidnapping nm

Un kilo nm | *A kilo*

Un kit nm

Un kiwi nm | *A kiwi*

Un koala nm | *A koala*

L

La pr | *Her - It*

Un laboratoire nm | *A laboratory*

Un lac nm | *A lake*

Lâche adj | *Coward*

Laid adj | *Ugly*

Une laisse nf | *A leash*

Le lait nm | *Milk*

Du lait d'amande nm | *Almond milk*

Une lampe nf | *The lamp*

Une langue nf | *A language*

La langue officielle nf | *The official language*

Un lapin nm | *A rabbit*

Un laptop nm

La laque nf | *Hairspray*

Un laser nm

Un lave-linge nm | *A washing machine*

Un lave-vaisselle nm | *A dishwasher*

Laver v | *To wash*

Une leçon nf | *A lesson*

La lecture nf | *Reading*

Léger - Légère adj | *Light*

Un legging nm | *A pair of leggings*

Des légumes nm | *Vegetables*

Le lendemain de | *The day after (in the future)*

Le lendemain matin | *The next morning*

Lent - Lente adj | *Slow*

La lessive nf | *The laundry*

Une lettre nf | *A letter*

Leur adj | *Their*

Les lèvres nf | *Lips*

Un lézard nm | *A lizard*

Un - Une libraire n | *A bookseller*

Une librairie nf | *A bookstore*

Libre adj | *Free*

Un lien nm | *A link*

Une lime nf | *A file*

Lire v | *To read*

Un lit nm | *A bed*

Un litchi nm | *A lychee*

Un litchi nm | *A lychee tree*

La litière nf | *Litter*

Un litre nm | *A liter*

Un living room nm

Un livre nm | *A book*

Une livre de nf | *A pound of*

Un logiciel nm | *A software*

Long - Longue adj | *Long*

Un losange nm | *A diamond*

Une louche nf | A ladle
Louer v | To rent
Un loup nm | A wolf
Lourd - Lourde adj | Heavy
Low-cost adj
Lundi nm | Monday
La Lune nf | The Moon
Des lunettes nf | Glasses
Des lunettes de soleil nf | Sunglasses
Un lynx nm | A lynx

M

La mâchoire nf | Jaw
Un magasin nm | A shop
Un magasin de chaussures nm | A shoe store
Un magasin de jouets nm | A toy store
Un magasin de musique nm | A music store
Un magasin de seconde main nm |
A thrift store
Un magasin de spiritueux nm | A liquor store
Un magasin de sport nm | A sports store
Un magasin de vêtements nm |
A clothes store
Un magicien nm | A magician
Un magazine nm | A magazine
Mai nm | May
Un maillot de bain nm | A swimsuit
La main nf | Hand
Maintenant adv | Now
Le maire nm | Mayor
Mais conj | But
Du maïs nm | Corn
La maison nf | The house
Le maître nm | Master
Le majeur nm | Middle finger
Mal adj | Wrong
Mal taillé(e) | Badly cut
Malade adj | Sick
Un mâle nm | A male
Une malle nf | A trunk
Un mammifère nm | A mammal

Un manager nm
Manger v | To eat
Une mangue nf | A mango
Un manguier nm | A mango tree
Une manique nf | An oven mit
Un manuel nm | A textbook
Un manuel scolaire nm | A textbook
Marcher v | To walk
Mardi nm | Tuesday
Un mari nm | A husband
Mariner v | To marinate
Le marketing nm
Une marraine nf | A godmother
Mars nm | March
Un masque nm | A mask
Un match nm
Une matière nf | A subject
Un matin nm | A morning
Mauvais - Mauvaise adj | Bad
Les mauvaises herbes nf | Weeds
De la mayonnaise nf | Mayonnaise
Un mécanicien - Une mécanicienne n |
A mechanic
Méchant - Méchante adj | Mean
Des mèches nf | Highlights
Mécontent - Mécontente adj | Unhappy
Un - Une médecin n | A doctor
Un meeting nm
Mélanger v | To blend - To mix
Un melon nm | A melon
Un mémoire nm | A thesis
La mémoire nf | The memory
Le menton nm | Chin
Un menuisier - Une menuisière n |
A carpenter
La menuiserie nf | Woodworking
La mer nf | Sea
Mercredi nm | Wednesday
Une mère nf | A mother
Mes adj | My
Mesurer v | To measure
La météo nf | The weather

Une méthode nf | *A method*
Un mètre nm | *A meter*
Le métro nm | *The subway*
Un mets nm | *A dish - A delicacy*
Mettre v | *To put*
Le Mexique nm | *Mexico*
Miauler v | *To meow*
Un micro-ondes nm | *A microwave*
Un (four à) micro-ondes nm |
A microwave oven
Midi nm | *Noon*
Du miel nm | *Honey*
Un millénaire nm | *A millennium*
Un milliard nm | *A billion*
Un milligramme nm | *A milligram*
Un millilitre nm | *A milliliter*
Mijoter v | *To simmer*
Minuit nm | *Midnight*
Une minute nf | *A minute*
Mixer v | *To mix*
Un mixeur nm | *A blender*
Un mois nm | *A month*
Le mois de ... | *The month of*
Les mois de l'année | *Months of the year*
Le mois dernier | *Last month*
Le mois prochain | *Next month*
Le mollet nm | *Calf*
Mon adj | *My*
Le monde nm | *The world*
Le mont nm | *Mountain*
Le mont Everest nm | *Mount Everest*
Monter v | *To assemble*
Monter dans le train | *To get on the train*
Un morceau de nm | *A piece of*
Un mot de passe nm | *A password*
Un motel nm | *A motel*
Une moto nf | *A motorcycle*
Les mots croisés nm | *Crosswords*
Mou - Molle | *Soft*
Une moufette nf | *A skunk*
Les moustaches nf | *Whiskers*
La moustache nf | *Moustache*

De la moutarde nf | *Mustard*
Un mouton nm | *A sheep*
Mûr adj | *Ripe*
Un mur nm | *A wall*
Une mûre nf | *A mulberry*
Un murier nm | *A mulberry bush*
Le museau nm | *Nose*
Un musée nm | *A museum*
Un musicien - Une musicienne n | *A musician*
De la musique nf | *Music*
Une myrtille nf | *A blueberry*
Un myrtillier nm | *A blueberry bush*

N

Une nappe nf | *A tablecloth*
Une narine nf | *A nostril*
Naturel - Naturelle adj | *Natural*
Une navette nf | *A shuttle*
Un navigateur nm | *A browser*
Naviguer v | *To navigate*
La neige nf | *Snow*
Nettoyer v | *To clean*
Un neveu nm | *A nephew*
Les news nf
Le nez nm | *Nose*
Ni conj | *Neither*
Une nièce nf | *A niece*
Une niche nf | *A niche*
Un nid nm | *A nest*
Un niveau nm | *A level*
Noir - Noire adj | *Black*
Une noix de coco nf | *A coconut*
Un nom d'utilisateur nm | *A username*
Le nombril nm | *Belly button*
Non-stop adj
Une note nf | *A grade*
Une notice nf | *Medicine instructions*
De la nourriture nf | *Food*
Nouveau - Nouvelle adj | *New*
Les nouvelles nf | *The news*
Novembre nm | *November*

Un nœud nm | *A bow*
Une nuit nf | *A night*

O

Obéir v | *To obey*
Obéissant - Obéissante adj | *Obedient*
Obtenir v | *To get*
Occupé - Occupée adj | *Busy*
Octobre nm | *October*
Un oignon nm | *An onion*
Un octogone nm | *An octagon*
Offrir v | *To give*
Une olive nf | *An olive*
Un olivier nm | *An olive tree*
Un oncle nm | *An uncle*
Les ongles nm | *Nails*
Open adj
Orange adj | *Orange*
Une orange nf | *An orange*
Un oranger nm | *An orange tree*
Un ordinateur nm | *A computer*
Un ordinateur de bureau nm | *A desktop*
Un ordinateur portable nm | *A laptop*
Les oreilles nf | *Ears*
Les organes génitaux nm | *Genitals*
Les organes vitaux nm | *Vital organs*
Organisé - Organisée adj | *Organized*
Organiser v | *To organize*
Un os nm | *A bone*
Ou conj | *Or*
Où pr | *Where*
L'ouest nm | *West*
Un ours nm | *A bear*
Ouvert - Ouverte adj | *Open*
Un ouvre-boîtes nm | *A can opener*
Un ouvrier - Une ouvrière n | *A laborer*
Un ovale nm | *An oval*
De l'oxygène nf | *Oxygen*
L'œil - Les yeux nm | *Eye(s)*
Des œufs nm | *Eggs*

P

Un pacemaker nm
Une page nf | *A page*
Une paie nf | *A pay*
Un pain nm | *A loaf of bread*
Un pair nm | *A peer*
Pair adj | *Even*
Une paire nf | *A pair*
La paix nf | *Peace*
Le pancréas nm | *Pancreas*
Un panier nm | *A dog bed*
Un pantalon nm | *Pants*
Une papaye nf | *A papaya*
Un papayer nm | *A papaya tree*
Un papillon nm | *A butterfly*
Un paquet de nm | *A pack of - A bag of*
Par prep | *By*
Un parallélogramme nm | *A parallelogram*
Un parasol nm | *An umbrella*
Les parents nm | *The parents*
Un parking nm
Parler v | *To speak*
Un parrain nm | *A godfather*
Partager v | *To share*
Une part nf | *A part*
Un parti nm | *A political party*
Participer v | *To participate*
Une partie nf | *A game*
Partir v | *To leave*
Partir en vacances | *To go on vacation*
Un passager - Une passagère n | *A passenger*
Un passeport nm | *A passport*
Passer du temps | *To spend time*
Une passoire nf | *A strainer*
Une pastèque nf | *A watermelon*
La pâte nf | *Dough*
De la pâtée nf | *Wet food*
Des pâtes nf | *Pasta*
Une pâtisserie nf | *A bakery*
Un pâtissier - Une pâtissière n | *A pastry chef*
Une patte nf | *A paw*

La **paume** nf | *Palm*

Pauvre adj | *Poor*

Un **pays** nm | *A country*

Une **pêche** nf | *A peach*

Un **pêcher** nm | *A peach tree*

Un **peigne** nm | *A comb*

La **peinture** nf | *Painting*

Un - Une **peintre** n | *A painter*

Une **pelouse** nf | *A lawn*

Un **pentagone** nm | *A pentagon*

Le **père** nm | *Father*

Une **permanente** nf | *A perm*

Un **perroquet** nm | *A parrot*

Une **personne** nf | *A person*

Peser v | *To weigh*

Un **pet** nm | *A fart*

Petit - Petite adj | *Short*

Le **petit déjeuner** nm | *Breakfast*

Un **petit-fils** nm | *A grandson*

Les **petits-enfants** nm | *The grandchildren*

Une **petite-fille** nf | *A granddaughter*

Un **petit magasin** nm | *A convenience store*

Des **petits pois** nm | *Garden peas*

La **peur** nf | *Fear*

Une **phalange** nf | *A phalanx*

Une **planche à découper** nf | *A cutting board*

Un **phare** nm | *A lighthouse*

Un **pharmacien - Une pharmacienne** n | *A pharmacist*

Une **pharmacie** nf | *A pharmacy*

La **philatélie** nf | *Stamp collecting*

Une **photo** nf | *A picture*

Une **photo de couverture** nf | *A cover picture*

Une **photo de profil** nf | *A profile picture*

Un - Une **photographe** n | *A photographer*

La **photographie** nf | *Photography*

Un **pickpocket** nm

Le **pied** nm | *Foot*

Piloter un avion | *To fly a plane*

Un **pin** nm | *A pine tree*

Des **pinces** nf | *Clips*

Un **pinguoin** nm | *A penguin*

Une **piscine** nm | *A pool*

Une **pizzéria** nf | *A pizza parlor*

Un **placard** nm | *A closet*

La **plage** nf | *The beach*

Une **planète** nf | *A planet*

Le **planning** nm

La **plante du pied** nf | *Base of the foot*

Planter v | *To plant*

Une **playlist** nf

Plein - Pleine adj | *Full*

Pleurer v | *To cry*

Plier v | *To fold*

Un **plombier - Une plombière** n | *A plumber*

Le **plus petit** | *The smallest*

Une **poêle** nf | *A pan - A skillet*

Un **poêle** nm | *A stove*

Un **poème** nm | *A poem*

Le **poignet** nm | *Wrist*

Le **poids** nm | *Weight*

Un **poil** nm | *A hair*

Le **poing** nm | *Fist*

Un **point** nm | *A point*

Les **pointes** nf | *The end*

Une **pointure** nf | *A shoesize*

Un **pois** nm | *A pea*

Un **poisson** nm | *A fish*

Un **poisson rouge** nm | *A goldfish*

Une **poire** nf | *A pear*

Du **poireau** nm | *Leek*

Un **poirier** nm | *A pear tree*

La **poitrine** nf | *Chest*

Un **poivrier** nm | *A pepper shaker*

Le **pôle Nord** nm | *The North Pole*

Poli - Polie | *Polite*

Un **policier - Une policière** n | *A police officer*

Les **polygones** nm | *Polygons*

Une **pomme** nf | *An apple*

Un **pommier** nm | *An apple tree*

Un - Une **pompier** n | *A firefighter*

Un **poney** nm | *A pony*

Le **pop-corn** nm

La **population mondiale** nf | *The world population*

Le **porc** nm | *Pork*

Un port nm | *A port*
Porter v | *To wear*
Porter à ébullition v | *To bring to a boil*
Un post nm
Un poste de police nm | *A police station*
Poster v | *To post*
Un pot de nm | *A jar of*
Un potager nm | *A vegetable garden*
La poterie nf | *Pottery*
Une poubelle nf | *A trash bin*
Le pouce nm | *Thumb*
Une poule nf | *A hen*
Les poumons nm | *Lungs*
Pousser v | *To grow*
Un poussin nm | *A chick*
Préchauffer v | *To preheat*
Préférer v | *To prefer*
Le premier homme | *The first man*
Prendre v | *To take*
Prendre v | *To have*
Prendre des photos | *To take photos*
Prendre la voiture | *To take the car*
Prendre le bus | *To take the bus*
Prendre le train | *To take the train*
Prendre soin de | *To take care of*
Prendre son petit déjeuner |
To have breakfast
Prendre un bain | *To take a bath*
Prendre un vol | *To take a flight*
Prendre une douche | *To take a shower*
Préparer v | *To prepare*
Préparer ses affaires | *To prepare things*
Près adv | *Near*
Prêt adj | *Ready*
Le printemps nm | *Spring*
Une prison nf | *A jail*
Les proches nm | *Relatives*
La production nf | *Production*
Produire v | *To produce*
Un professeur - Une professeure n | *A teacher*
Un profil nm | *A profile*
Des progrès nm | *Progress*
Une promenade nf | *A walk*

Promener le chien v | *To walk the dog*
Propre adj | *Clean*
Un prospectus nm | *A flyer*
Une prune nf | *A plum*
Un prunier nm | *A plum tree*
Un - Une psychologue n | *A psychologist*
Une publication nf | *A post*
Publier v | *To publish*
Un pull nm | *A sweater*
Un puzzle nm | A puzzle
Un pyjama nm | *A pajamas*
Une pyramide nf | *A pyramid*

Q

Quand adv | *When*
Quant prep | *As for*
Un quart nm | *A quarter*
Un quart d'heure nm | *A quarter of an hour*
Une question nf | *A question*
La queue nf | *Tail*
Quel temps fait-il ? | *How is the weather?*

R

Une race nf | *A breed*
Rafraîchir v | *To refresh*
Ramasser les feuilles | *To pick up leaves*
La randonnée nf | *Hiking*
Une randonnée nf | *A hike*
Ranger v | *To tidy*
Râper v | *To grate*
Rapide adj | *Fast*
Un rasoir électrique nm | *An electric razor*
Un rasoir nm | *A razor*
Un raton laveur nm | *A raccoon*
Une rayure nf | *A stripe*
Réagir v | *To react*
Une recette nf | *A recipe*
Recevoir v | *To receive*
Recevoir v | *To entertain*
Une recherche nf | *Research*

Récolter v | *To harvest*
Recommander v | *To recommend*
Un rectangle nm | *A rectangle*
Redémarrer v | *To restart*
Réduire v | *To reduce*
Un réfrigérateur nm | *A refrigerator*
Regarder v | *To watch*
Regarder la télévision | *To watch TV*
Une règle nf | *A rule*
Les reins nm | *Kidneys*
Remplir v | *To fill*
Remuer v | *To blend - To mix*
Un renard nm | *A fox*
Un rendez-vous nm | *An appointment*
Rendre visite v | *To visit*
Rentrer v | *To come home*
Un repas nm | *A meal*
Répondre v | *To answer*
Une réponse nf | *A response*
Un réseau social nm | *A social media*
Réserver v | *To book*
Réserver un taxi | *To book a taxi*
Un restaurant nm | *A restaurant*
Un restaurant nm | *A restaurant*
Retourner v | *To return*
Un réveil nm | *An alarm clock*
Une révision nf | *A review*
Riche adj | *Rich*
Une ride nf | *A wrinkle*
Des rideaux nm | *Curtains*
Rincer v | *To rinse*
Un road trip nm | *A road trip*
Une robe nf | *A dress*
Un robinet nm | *A faucet*
Les rois nm | *Kings*
Un roman nm | *A novel*
Ronronner v | *To pur*
Rose adj | *Pink*
Le rose nm | *Pink*
Une rose nf | *A rose*
Rôtir v | *To roast*
Rouge adj | *Red*
Le rouge nm | *Red*

Roux adj | *Red*
Roux - Rousse adj | *Red-headed*

S

S'abonner v | *To subscribe*
S'amuser v | *To have a good time*
S'épiler v | *To pluck - To wax*
S'habiller v | *To get dressed*
S'hydrater v | *To hydrate*
S'occuper du jardin | *To take care of the yard*
Sa adj | *Her - His - Its*
Un sac de plage nm | *A beach bag*
Un safari nm | *A safari*
Sain - Saine adj | *Healthy*
Les saisons nf | *Seasons*
La Saint-Valentin nf | *Valentine's Day*
Salé - Salée adj | *Salty*
Sale adj | *Dirty*
Une salière nf | *A saltshaker*
La salle à manger nf | *The dining room*
Une salle de bain nf | *A bathroom*
Une salle de classe nf | *A classroom*
Une salle de jeux nf | *A playroom*
Un salon nm | *A living room*
Un salon de coiffure nm | *A hairdresser*
Samedi nm | *Saturday*
Des sandales nf | *Sandals*
Un sandwich nm
Le sang nm | *Blood*
Un sanglier nm | *A wild boar*
Sans prep | *Without*
Saoul adj | *Drunk*
De la sauce piquante nf | *Hot sauce*
De la sauce soja nf | *Soy sauce*
Un saut nm | *A jump*
Sauvegarder v | *To save*
Savoir v | *To know*
Le savon nm | *Soap*
Un sceau nm | *A stamp*
Les sciences nf | *Sciences*
Un scooter nm | *A scooter*
Un script nm | *A script*

La sculpture nf | *Sculpting*

Se pr | *Themselves*

Se brosser les cheveux | *To brush one's hair*

Se brosser les dents | *To brush one's teeth*

Se brosser v | *To brush*

Se changer v | *To get changed*

Se connecter v | *To log in*

Se coucher v | *To set*

Se couvrir v | *To cover up*

Se déconnecter v | *To log out*

Se démaquiller v | *To remove makeup*

Se désabonner v | *To unsubscribe*

Se déshabiller v | *To undress*

Se déshydrater v | *To dehydrate*

Se laver les cheveux | *To wash your hair*

Se laver v | *To wash yourself*

Se lever v | *To get up*

Se maquiller v | *To make up*

Se préparer v | *To get ready*

Se raser v | *To shave*

Se situer v | *To be located*

Se trouver v | *To be located*

Un seau nm | *A bucket*

Sec - Sèche adj | *Dry*

Un sèche-cheveux nm | *A hairdryer*

Un sèche-linge nm | *A dryer*

Une seconde nf | *A second*

Un - Une secrétaire n | *A secretary*

Le sein nm | *Breast*

Le self-service nm

Un selfie nm

Une semaine nf | *A week*

La semaine dernière | *Last week*

La semaine prochaine | *Next week*

Semer v | *To seed*

Un semestre nm | *A semester*

Sentir bon | *To smell good*

Un seprent nm | *A snake*

Septembre nm | *September*

Un serial killer nm

Une série télévisée nf | *A TV Series*

Servir v | *To serve*

Une serviette nf | *A napkin*

Une serviette de plage nf | *A beach towel*

Un serveur - Une serveuse n | *A waiter*

Le shampoing nm | *Shampoo*

Le shopping nm | *Shopping*

Un short nm | *A pair of shorts*

Un show nm

Un siècle nm | *A century*

Le signe nm | *Sign*

Silencieux - Silencieuse adj | *Silent*

Le sirop d'érable nm | *Maple syrup*

Un site internet nm | *A website*

Un sketch nm

Un smartphone nm

Un soldat - Une soldate n | *A soldier*

Le soleil nm | *The sun*

La soif nf | *Thirst*

Une soirée nf | *An evening*

Un sommet nm | *A peak*

Sortir v | *To take out*

Un sou nm | *A penny*

Souffler v | *To blow*

Une soupe aux poireaux nf | *A leek soup*

Les sourcils nm | *Eyebrows*

Une souris nf | *A mouse*

Sous prep | *Under*

Un souvenir nm | *A memory*

Un souvenir nm | *A souvenir*

Une sœur nf | *A sister*

Un spam nm

Une spatule nf | *A spatula*

Une sphère nf | *A sphere*

Du sport nm | *Sport*

Le sport - L'exercice nm | *Exercising*

Un stage nm | *An internship*

Une star nf

Une station d'essence nf | *A petrol station - A gas station*

La Statue de la Liberté nf | *The Statue of Liberty*

Un sticker nm

Un stop nm | *A stop*

Une story nf | *A story*

Stressant - Stressante adj | *Stressful*

Un succès nm | *A success*
Sucré - Sucrée adj | *Sweet*
Le sud nm | *South*
Suer v | *To sweat*
Un sujet nm | *A topic*
Suivre v | *To follow*
Un supermarché nm | *A supermarket*
Un supporter nm
Une surprise nf | *A surprise*
Sympathique adj | *Friendly*
Le système solaire nm | *Solar system*

T

Un t-shirt nm | *A t-shirt*
Une table nf | *A table*
Une table de cuisine nf | *A kitchen table*
Une table d'extérieur nf | *An outdoor table*
Une tablette de nf | *A bar of*
Un tableau nm | *A blackboard/whiteboard*
Un tableau nm | *A painting*
Tailler v | *To trim*
Tailler les haies | *To trim the hedges*
Le talon nm | *Heel*
Un t-shirt nm | *A t-shirt*
Une taille nf | *A size*
Une tante nf | *An aunt*
Taper v | *To type*
Un tapis nm | *A carpet*
Un tapis de souris nm | *A mouse pad*
Tard adv | *Late*
Une tasse nf | *A cup*
Une tasse de nf | *A cup of*
Un taureau nm | *A bull*
Un taxi nm | *A taxi*
Un teaser nm
Télécharger v | *To download*
Un téléphérique nm | *A cable car*
Un téléphone nm | *A phone*
La télévision nf | *TV*
Le temps nm | *The weather*
Une tendance nf | *A trend*
Le tennis nm

Une tente nf | *A tent*
Une terrasse nm | *A patio*
La Terre nf | *Earth*
Terrestre adj | *Land*
Une théière nf | *A teapot*
Un thriller nm
Le thon nm | *Tuna*
Un tic nm | *A tic*
Le timing nm
Une tique nf | *A tick*
Les toilettes nf | *A toilet - A powder room*
Ton adj | *Your*
Un ton nm | *A tone*
Tondre v | *To mow*
Tondre la pelouse | *To mow the lawn*
Des tongs nf | *Flip-flops*
Une tondeuse nf | *A lawn mower*
Une tonne nf | *A ton*
Un top nm | *A top*
Le torse nm | *Torso*
Une tortue nf | *A turtle*
Tôt adv | *Early*
Une tour nf | *A tower*
La Tour de Pise nf | *The Leaning Tower*
La tour Eiffel nf | *The Eiffel Tower*
Tourner v | *To turn*
Une traduction nf | *A translation*
Un train nm | *A train*
Un train à grande vitesse (TGV) nm | *A high-speed train*
Un traitement nm | *A treatment*
Un tramway nm | *A streetcar*
Une tranche de nf | *A slice of*
Trancher v | *To slice*
Un trapèze nm | *A trapezoid*
Le travail nm | *Work*
Travailler v | *To work*
Tremper v | *To soak*
Un triangle nm | *A triangle*
Un tribunal nm | *Court*
Le tricot nm | *Knitting*
Un trimestre nm | *A trimester*
Des triplés nm | *Triplets*

Triste adj | *Sad*
La tristesse nf | *Sadness*
Trop grand - grande | *Too big - too large*
Trop petit - petite | *Too small*
Une trottinette nf | *A scooter*
La truffe nf | *Dog's nose*

U

Une université nf | *A university*
Une usine nf | *A factory*
Utile adj | *Useful*
Un utilisateur - Une utilisatrice n | *A user*
Utiliser du fil dentaire | *To floss*

V

Les vacances nf | *Vacations*
Une vache nf | *A cow*
Vain adj | *Superficial*
La vaisselle nf | *Dishes*
Une valise nf | *A suitcase*
Un veau nm | *A calf*
La veille de | *The day before (in the past)*
Un vélo nm | *A bicycle*
Un vélo électrique nm | *An electric bike*
Un vendeur - Une vendeuse n |
A shop assistant
Vendredi nm | *Friday*
Le ventre nm | *Stomach*
Un ventilateur nm | *A fan*
Un ver nm | *A worm*
Une véranda nf | *A solarium*
Vérifier v | *To verify*
Un verre nm | *A glass*
Un verre à vin nm | *A wine glass*
Un verre de nm | *A glass of*
Verrouiller v | *To lock*
Vers prep | *Toward*
Un vers nm | *A verse*
Verser v | *To pour*
Vert - Verte adj | *Green*

La vessie nf | *Bladder*
De la viande nf | *Meat*
Vide adj | *Empty*
Une vidéo nf | *A video*
Vieux - Vieille adj | *Old*
Le vin nm | *Wine*
Du vin blanc nm | *White wine*
Du vin rouge nm | *Red wine*
De la vinaigrette nf | *Salad dressing*
Vingt n | *Twenty*
Vintage adj
Violet - Violette adj | *Violet - Purple*
Un visa nm | *A visa*
Visible adj | *Visible*
Une visite nf | *A tour*
Visiter v | *To visit*
Vivre v | *To live*
Le vocabulaire nm | *Vocabulary*
Voir v | *To see*
Un voisin nm | *Dinner*
Une voiture nf | *A car*
Une volaille nf | *Poultry*
Voler v | *To fly*
Voyager v | *To travel*
Un vœu nm | *A wish*
Vu prep | *Given*
La vue nf | *Sight*

W

Le week-end nm
Un workshop nm

Y

Des yaourts nm | *Yogurts*

Z

Un zèbre nm | *A zebra*

THANK YOU

Thank you for choosing the **_French Vocabulary Workbook_** as your language-learning companion. I sincerely hope that it helped you improve your French vocabulary and understanding of the language in general.

My goal with this book was to provide daily activities for you to learn more French vocabulary related to daily situations. As always, I would greatly appreciate your feedback, so please consider leaving a review where you purchased this workbook.

I always create content for French learners on my YouTube channel, Instagram, or website. You can find all my resources and links at www.theperfectfrench.com.

I hope you found this workbook helpful in your language-learning journey.

Once again, thank you for choosing the **_French Vocabulary Workbook_**. I wish you all the best in your progress toward becoming more fluent in French every day!

Dylane

MY BOOKS

The Complete French Courses – Including books, videos, and audio.

> **The Complete French Pronunciation Course**
> **The Complete French Conjugation Course**
> **The Complete French Grammar Course**
> **The Complete French Vocabulary Course**
> **The Complete French Expressions Course**

Conjugation Textbooks – Including books, video, and audio.

> **Passé Composé vs Imparfait**
> **The French Subjunctive**

The French Short Stories – Including books and audio.

> **French Short Stories – Volume 1**
> **French Short Stories – Volume 2**
> **French Long Stories – Volume 3**

My Free Self-Study Guide – Including all my lessons listed and my study plan.

> **The Complete French Self-Study Guide**

Download my free self-study guide at **www.theperfectfrench.com/freebies**.